Career Management

Patrick Forsyth

- *The* fast track route to jump-starting your career and maximising your success

- Covers key career management techniques, from lifelong learning to getting promoted, and from surviving office politics to goal setting

- Packed with lessons and tips from great careers and ideas from leading thinkers like Charles Handy

- Includes a glossary of key concepts and a comprehensive resources guide

>EXPRESS EXEC.COM<
essential management thinking at your fingertips

LIFE & WORK

10.03

The right of Patrick Forsyth to be identified as the author of this work has been asserted in accordance with the Copyright, Designs and Patents Act 1988

First published 2002 by
Capstone Publishing (A Wiley Company)
8 Newtec Place
Magdalen Road
Oxford OX4 1RE
United Kingdom
http://www.capstoneideas.com

CIP catalogue records for this book are available from the British Library and the US Library of Congress

ISBN 1-84112-192-4

Printed and bound by CPI Antony Rowe, Eastbourne

This book is printed on acid-free paper

Substantial discounts on bulk quantities of Capstone books are available to corporations, professional associations and other organizations. Please contact Capstone for more details on +44 (0)1865 798 623 or (fax) +44 (0)1865 240 941 or (e-mail) info@wiley-capstone.co.uk

Contents

Introduction to ExpressExec   v

10.03.01 Introduction to Career Management   1
10.03.02 What is Career Management?   5
10.03.03 The Evolution of Career Management   11
10.03.04 The E-Dimension   19
10.03.05 The Global Dimension   27
10.03.06 The State of the Art   37
10.03.07 In Practice   53
10.03.08 Key Concepts and Thinkers   71
10.03.09 Resources   79
10.03.10 Ten Steps to Making Career Management Work   89

Frequently Asked Questions (FAQs)   101
Acknowledgments   103
Index   105

Introduction to ExpressExec

ExpressExec is 3 million words of the latest management thinking compiled into 10 modules. Each module contains 10 individual titles forming a comprehensive resource of current business practice written by leading practitioners in their field. From brand management to balanced scorecard, ExpressExec enables you to grasp the key concepts behind each subject and implement the theory immediately. Each of the 100 titles is available in print and electronic formats.

Through the ExpressExec.com Website you will discover that you can access the complete resource in a number of ways:

» printed books or e-books;
» e-content – PDF or XML (for licensed syndication) adding value to an intranet or Internet site;
» a corporate e-learning/knowledge management solution providing a cost-effective platform for developing skills and sharing knowledge within an organization;
» bespoke delivery – tailored solutions to solve your need.

Why not visit www.expressexec.com and register for free key management briefings, a monthly newsletter and interactive skills checklists. Share your ideas about ExpressExec and your thoughts about business today.

Please contact elound@wiley-capstone.co.uk for more information.

Introduction to Career Management

Why is career management a must in today's volatile world of work? This chapter sets the scene and explains the importance to everyone.

» Success ahead? Career development for the new millennium
» The way ahead

"Some people are better than others at anticipating the response of a complex environment, and it is people with this ability that are likely, in the long run, to be most successful."

Mark Casson, Professor of Economics, Reading University

SUCCESS AHEAD? CAREER DEVELOPMENT FOR THE NEW MILLENNIUM

Unless you have the luxury of not having to work, your work is likely to be a major part of your life. Thus most people want two things from this: rewards (essentially financial reward) and job satisfaction. If you are going to spend a major part of your life working, then it is surely best to do something you like. Remember what the journalist Katherine Whitehorn said: *"The best career advice to give the young is: find out what you like doing and get someone to pay you for doing it"* – perhaps good advice at any age.

We do not choose and undertake our work in a vacuum, of course. Decisions need to be made in the context of the broader world. And this broader world of work has changed radically in the last decade. As the twenty-first century gets underway, any individual is right to wonder how their career will progress and whether it will give them what they want. Uncertainty is the order of the day. Many may feel they remember "better times," that is, times when there was more certainty about how a career would progress. Many organizations had planned career paths for people and, although progress varied somewhat, once on a path the direction in which you would be able to go was reasonably clear. In some industries this was particularly true. Banks make a good example, yet banks have changed too, and more than many kinds of organization.

Some may hanker for these "better days," but waiting for things to return to normal is simply not one of the options. There are currently few, if any, safe havens, and few, if any, organizations that seem likely to be so again in the near future.

Despite all this you no doubt want to thrive, prosper, and get on; and you probably want to enjoy your job while you do so. So what is the moral? How can you ensure that you do well? The simple answer is that there is nothing you can do that will *guarantee* success (if there ever was). But there is a great deal you can do to make success more likely. And this is what this work is about.

THE WAY AHEAD

Let us be clear: this is not a guide to how to apply for a new job successfully, though it touches on some of the issues. Nor is it a guide to *career planning and development* in the corporate sense, that is, it is not about how a company may organize career paths for people, or at least for some people, though again this is mentioned.

Rather, it is about *career management* in the sense of the analysis, planning, and action that can be taken by an individual at any stage of their career – and ideally throughout it – to *actively* increase the chances of their doing well. The concept of it being an *active* process is key. For the most part, success comes not to those who sit and wait, nor even to those who take advantages of opportunities as they may occur, though this should be part of it. Success has to be *actively* sought. In today's volatile and competitive world of work perhaps "*very* actively sought" puts it better. What is more, you have to have a clear idea of what you mean by "success" to have any chance of moving purposely towards it. So defining goals, financial and of every other sort, is inherent to the process.

For the successful careerist this means a number of things. You must adopt the right attitudes, study and analyze the area and circumstances in which you work, plan and implement action to assist your progress. You need to be quick on your feet, ready for anything so that you can adjust longer-term plans tactically and fine-tune your actions as necessary.

You need to have the management of your career in mind constantly. There will rarely, if ever, be stages where you can rest on your laurels, and while it must not distract you from doing a good job – this is, after all, one of the things that assists success – career management must become a regular part of your thinking. Your career is affected by everything you do – and by everything and everyone around you. The world and other people around you are not necessarily all on your side. The stage on which your career is acted out is a competitive arena, and a constructive attitude is necessary therefore to combat possible difficulties along your career path as well as to do the positive things that will take you forward.

While there are more chrysalises than butterflies, flying free is worth the effort.

What is Career Management?

Defining the process and highlighting the practical implications and opportunities stemming from it, this chapter provides a foundation for positive action.

- » Responses to change
- » Career management defined
- » The fundamentals of career management
- » The concept of career skills
- » The way ahead
- » Summary

"Success means accomplishments as a result of our own efforts and abilities. Proper preparation is the key to our success. Our acts can be no wiser than our thoughts. Our thinking can be no wiser than our thoughts. Our thinking can be no wiser than our understanding."

George S. Clason, publisher and author

First, it may be worth asking an obvious question just to set the record straight. What is a job? In *The Human Side of Organizations*[1] it is defined thus: "To many people a job is an identity. To managers a job is a collection of tasks. In the past, this question probably did not need to be answered. Historically, jobs were perceived as the property of employers. The legal term for this is employment at will. This means people are hired and retained according to the will of the employer. It also means that both the employer and the employee are free to separate at any time with no advance warning. In the past, this has been more of an advantage for employers than employees."

Whatever your work involves, it takes place in real time and in the real world. Business pundits and economists predict a range of varying scenarios for the future of the work environment. But one thing they are *all* certain about – it will be uncertain. We live in dynamic times. The old world of job security, jobs for life, prescribed ladders of promotion and gradually increasing success and rewards has gone, replaced by talk of downsizing (and calling it rightsizing makes it sound no better), redundancy, tele-working, and portfolio careers.

The reasons for the radical changes that have occurred in the world of work, especially over the last 20 years or so, are many. They include the information technology revolution, the increase in globalization, more competitive markets, and changes to the way modern, leaner, flatter organizations are organized and to the job structures that operate within them. A variety of difficulties, from rising oil prices and increasing legislation to overall economic problems and recessions, have prompted more change and accelerated the process. (For more detail, see Chapter 3, The Evolution of Career Management).

In case anyone feels left out, it should be noted that other kinds of organization, those that may not see themselves as "commercial" or which are non-profit-making (by intention, that is!), have changed almost as much. For those working in, say, a large charity or even a government body of some sort, their situation will be very like that of their more commercial peers. They will doubtless be busy, they may work long hours, resources may be limited, and it may be also that they suffer more stress; certainly they will be under some pressure to succeed in meeting whatever goals or targets their particular job entails.

Now, waiting for things to "get back to normal" is simply not one of the options. No one can guarantee a successful career for themselves, but its progress is something that everyone can influence to some degree. Indeed, it is something that you surely *want* to influence. We all spend a great deal of time at work. It is important to make sure that time is as enjoyable and rewarding as possible.

RESPONSES TO CHANGE

There is a line in one of the late John Lennon's songs: "Life is what happens while you are making other plans." It encapsulates a painful thought. There is perhaps no worse situation to get into than one where we look back and say to ourselves: "if only . . ."

So, with no rigid, preordained career ladder to follow, careers need planning. The question is how to do it. The bad news is that there is no magic formula. Sorry, but you cannot just snap your fingers, shout "Promotion!" and be made chief executive overnight (or if you can, please let me know how!). You can, however, make a difference if you work at it.

CAREER MANAGEMENT DEFINED

To define terms: *career management* is the active planning and implementation of strategy and action likely to assist in furthering your career. It is a process other people may assist, but which *only you* can initiate and direct. For the record and to avoid confusion, *career planning* is a term more usually used by an organization (together with phrases like *job succession*) to describe plans for members of staff. While such plans are certainly concerned with how people will progress through an organization, they are based on how the individual can assist the organization and not so much on what will best meet the individual's own personal objectives. Thus, even when this general area is addressed by an organization's policy and practice, the need for personal career management remains valid. Indeed, perhaps this makes it more important in such circumstances.

THE FUNDAMENTALS OF CAREER MANAGEMENT

The starting point to the career management process is your knowing what you want, and this needs some systematic self-analysis (more details of this are in Chapter 6, The State of the Art).

After some self-analysis, you can set clear objectives; the old adage that "if you do not know where you are going, any road will do" is nowhere more true. Career management means aiming high. You can always trade down a bit, but you may be more successful than you think, and it is a pity to miss achieving something not because it is unachievable, but only because you do not try for it.

From here on the management, and fine-tuning, of your career progress is in the details, and the first step is to realize just that so that you can work at them all. But there is one major factor to consider – progress is dependent, probably to a major degree, on job performance – on the achievement of results. Unless you "deliver," then you will have little chance of being judged able to cope with more responsibility, and promotion, or being able to move on, may – rightly – elude you.

THE CONCEPT OF CAREER SKILLS

What allows you to succeed? Not least important are the skills and competencies that you have. But they do not just help you do the job; many are so important that they deserve the name *career skills*. For example, how many people in business in the future will survive without, say, a modicum of computer skills? One could list many more skills that are mandatory in one job or another; and many too that are common to most jobs. In many executive or management jobs such skills include: all aspects of managing people, presentation and business writing and other communications skills, numeracy and (so often said these days) computer skills, and more general skills such as good time management.

Thus one area of active career management consists of recognizing what career skills can help you and making sure that you excel in them.

In addition, there are a host of other factors that have an influence on how you progress. Who you know is often quoted as being as important as what you know. Some people seem very well connected. But this does not just happen. They probably work at it: they note their contacts, they seek out new ones, they keep in touch, and they recognize that this is a two-way process. It helps, and is another example of the sort of thing that needs working on.

THE WAY AHEAD

Active careerists do not rely on good luck (this is more likely to be the reason your "competitors" in the organization are successful!). They do, however, take advantage of any good fortune that comes their way. And their planning and positive attitude to the process make it more likely that they spot opportunities and can do so.

What is necessary is an all-embracing approach to what is essentially a life-long campaign. Those who approach career management systematically, who leave no stone unturned, and who look at every detail of their work life in terms of the career implications of it, tend to do best. If they have thought through what they want to do and if they have clear objectives, then – while they may not achieve everything they want – they will get closer to their ideal. This is true whether you seek to make progress within one large organization, or whether you realistically see your employer changing several times as the years go by.

It is worth noting that this process does not take place on a level playing field. You may well be in competition with others, within your organization and without, some of whom may operate with a streak of ruthlessness. In addition, those who you meet "professionally" as it were (conducting selection interviews or heading committees considering promotions, for instance) are busy and have difficult jobs. Their responsibility is more to operate successfully – to appoint or promote the right people – than to be "fair" to you. Some prejudice exists too, some the occasional malicious racism or whatever, more just designed to make the job easier however unscientific it may be. So, for example, there are people convinced that to be successful you have to be over a certain height, under a certain weight or born Sagittarius (though as one such I *know* they are nature's aristocrats!). It pays to be realistic about such hazards.

For the most part, careers do not just happen, they are made. You can do worse than start a more active phase of career development by recognizing this and seeing your career as likely to be influenced primarily – by you.

SUMMARY

Ignoring the need for career management risks experiencing major, or significant, shortfalls in your career progress and in the satisfaction and rewards it brings you. Even small differences in action may make a significant change to what occurs.

The principles are simple:

» recognize the need for career management;
» apply the actions that constitute it systematically, consistently, and regularly; and
» give what you do a real edge, linking realistically to the situation in the world of work and in the particular organization for which you work.

Like so much else, with the principles stated, what makes the process work well is the way in which it is approached:

» *what* precisely is done; and
» *how* it is executed.

The potential here is considerable – a little time and thought can change your life for the better. Career management is the antidote to saying: "if only . . ." somewhere down the line.

NOTE

1 Drafke, M.W. and Kossen, S. (1998) *The Human Side of Organizations*, 7th edn. Addison-Wesley, Reading, MA.

The Evolution of Career Management

Why is career management more important now than in the past? This chapter reviews the evolution of the workplace and thus of the need for active career attention.

» Changes and trends
» Views versus treatment
» The results of change
» Summary

"Some people see the future as something that will eventually roll along to them, just like a train pulling into a station. They wait hopefully for this train to bring them what they wish for ... But the future is not like this. Just as our present is the result of our past, so our future will be the result of our present."

Anne Spencer Parry and Marjorie Pizer

As organizations have changed, so too has the way people must relate to them and work in them. In turn, so has the way people must plan and act if they want to get on in them.

For many years a career "in business" was something that could be easily predicted. Some people did better than average, or indeed were luckier than average, but for many people progress was not something that needed striving for to any significant extent. It occurred naturally. Of course, small things made a difference, but so too did time. There were many jobs, and many organizations, where the people with any sort of potential rose gradually through the ranks as a result of little more than doing a reasonable job and keeping their noses clean. Although this paints a simplified picture, it also contains real truth.

Organizations grew steadily, and such growth did not involve their changing very much in nature. The successful ones got larger, some combined or were taken over, but the situation for staff and managers stayed recognizably similar. However, in the last couple of decades, things began to change, and change radically.

Detailed chronology is not important here, nor is the distant past. Let us start 20 years back and examine developments that began in the early 1980s.

CHANGES AND TRENDS

The key changes to organizations occurring from that time on include the following.

» *Competition*: With burgeoning choice for customers and all the changes inherent in a market-led economy, competition began to intensify, and in many industries it became increasingly international. A variety of operational matters changed as this occurred: everything, from product development to delivery, speeded up, and growth became something that could no longer be taken for granted.

» *Cost increase*: Alongside increasing competition, costs began to increase disproportionately, a factor that was accelerated by certain economic pressures, for example the increasing price of fuel. There was a direct spin off here to the manner of organization. Multi-layered companies began to look to see who was doing what and whether people at every level were strictly necessary. Industry, bloated by past success, began to develop less costly ways of working.

» *Information technology*: Although we have still to see the much predicted "paperless office," the advances in computers and allied equipment and the processes that go with it have certainly wrought change. Communication has become easier, information used to direct the business more reliable and up to date, and there have been direct effects on jobs and productivity. Such changes are not all for the better, as anyone who has held on for long minutes struggling through an organization's labyrinthine telephone system only to be told "the computer is down" knows only too well. Nevertheless, working practices have certainly been changed.

» *Internal hierarchies*: Staff have had to become more self-sufficient (they have been "empowered" in the jargon), and organizations have become flatter as layers of management have been cut and different ways found of getting work done.

» *Economic difficulty*: The final catalyst to change cut in during the early nineties. Many western economies suffered recession, and this intensified competitive pressures, made cost-cutting not just attractive, but essential, and prompted more changes – and additions to the vocabulary as companies began to "downsize," or to give it its more palatable – but euphemistic – name, to "rightsize."

All these influences added to and affected one another and a more dynamic business environment became the norm. Change continues. Now, when management guru Tom Peters is quoted as saying "Tomorrow's organizations will be conjured up anew every day," most people understand – and many would claim to work for one just like that.

How does all this ongoing change affect people and their careers?

VIEWS VERSUS TREATMENT

People remain an organization's greatest asset; indeed, many organizations say just that as part of their visions or missions. Maxims abound, for example: "If you want 10 days of happiness, grow grain. If you want 10 years of happiness, grow a tree. If you want 100 years of happiness, grow people."[1]

The common sense view favors people and, in terms of staff, it makes sense for employers to look after them. Recruiting good people remains a priority. Training and development, though the amount done does – perhaps understandably – wax and wane with financial success or the lack of it, continues to be regarded as a "good thing" and is even more necessary than in the past in a more dynamic environment. Motivation receives its fair share of attention and management is now more consultative and sensitively applied than ever before. And yet this is not the full picture.

Consider the common nature of the following events.

» *Redundancy*: Laying people off, often an action of last resort in the past, is now a routine response to even small difficulties.
» *Cut-back*: There is much less perseverance nowadays; if something does not go right, it is cut out before it does more damage.
» *Closure*: Similarly, difficulty may result in whole operations, offices or factories being closed or moved. (Another result of the increasingly international nature of business: got a problem in the UK? – move the operation to Singapore or China.)
» *Stress*: Business has become more stressful, we are told. Certainly a whole industry of stress counselors and allied products has grown up to deal with it, so it must be real (though it is surely better avoided in the first place than treated once it has occurred).
» *Short-term contract*: People are contracted to do a job, a project, not for a career, often with little thought as to what they do thereafter – that is their problem.
» *Tele-working*: Where people work has changed too. Telephone a company in London and you find yourself talking to someone with a Scottish accent who tells you they are based in Glasgow, or working from home with a computer and telephone in a croft in the far – and low cost – north.

All these factors and more affect the world of work, and all make it somehow less certain for the individual. You do not know how long a job will last and how likely it is to change. Not every post is gone or reorganized in a moment, of course, but some are, and through the last 20 years people have changed their outlook.

They no longer assume permanence so readily as they did in the past. They expect and accept as part of the work pattern that they may change employers more often than would have once been the case, or engage in "portfolio careers." Of course, some people will still do the same job for 20 years, or a lifetime, but the likelihood has changed.

Two other changes are worth noting, both to do with the law.

» *Employment law*: Employment law has been extended over the years in many countries. The protection it provides is doubtless good (and it is considerable, so much so that it is said that in some places "you need influence at senior level to get fired!"). The downside, and this affects the way staff are seen, is that employers' costs increase with every new benefit, and some at least act to avoid them. For example, for every benefit added to maternity (or paternity, for that matter) situations that assist some new parent, somewhere else it is just that much harder to get employment if you are a woman of obvious child-bearing age.

» *Anti-discrimination legislation*: Similarly, minority groups of all sorts are now better protected, but the whole way in which this has been progressed seems to make employers more wary of getting locked into expensive obligations to staff.

Every social change that touches on employment also affects attitudes to careers and how they need to be managed. A few examples serve to illustrate:

» people marrying and having children later in life changes their needs at earlier ages;
» more couples where both are employed and bringing in higher family incomes;
» greater mobility amongst many people (and greater possibility for it, for example around Europe);
» more people completing higher education (which affects entry requirements for many jobs); and

» women increasingly breaching the so-called "glass ceiling" and the mix of the sexes in the workplace changing.

There are, and will be, more such factors, and the world of work seems set to be a changing place for a while yet.

THE RESULTS OF CHANGE

The processes described, and the reporting of them, have begun to educate people to the new realities, and their expectations have changed accordingly.

Parallel changes have both helped and hindered. The three examples that follow show the range of matters involved here.

» *Computer technology*: This has changed the process of applying for and obtaining a job. Even small matters are significant. Word-processing means that it is easier to produce a professional looking CV and covering letter, but perhaps a little more difficult for recruiters to differentiate between competing applications. Certainly following the good advice that there is "no such thing as a standard CV" and, if necessary, adapting every single one sent out, is now easier to follow.

» *Media*: This has grown ever more diverse. Few industries have one sole place where people advertise and look for jobs. The variety of potential sources is legion, with new technology meaning that there are now more than 5000 online recruitment agencies listed as dealing with executive and managerial jobs online in the UK alone.

» *The personnel function*: Using the term to incorporate personnel, human resources, and training and development departments, everything here has become more sophisticated. In part, bureaucracy is to blame and one change has begotten another. The law covering sex discrimination, for instance, has prompted changes in everything from application forms to exit interviews. While some of the changes here do not help in career terms, some do – certainly in many organizations there are many more people and resources that may, potentially at least, help.

SUMMARY

The net result of all this is that now, as we begin the twenty-first century, the implications for the ambitious careerist are clear.

» Career progress cannot be assumed.
» The work environment is dynamic and volatile and will remain so. "Waiting for things to get back to normal" is simply not an option.
» A professional and systematic approach to job finding, and to career planning and management is a necessity.
» Given the competitive environment within many organizations, handling matters to give yourself an edge is only prudent.
» Excellence in career management is as important as excellence in the performance of your job.

Nothing currently predicted seems to make any other view possible in the near future than that of viewing active career management as a necessity.

NOTE

1 Harvey Mackay, CEO of Mackay Envelope Company.

The E-Dimension

The information technology revolution seems to affect everything, and careers are no exception. This chapter investigates how these new developments sit alongside the age-old need for success at work.

» Negative impact on jobs
» Positive impact on jobs
» Changes to being employed
» The rise of knowledge
» Changes to making progress
» Changes to finding employment
» Best practice

"Technology is important but not a solution unto itself. It offers different things to different people. Individual users want technology to make their jobs easier. Managers want technology to make their staff more productive. Corporate officers want technology to make them more competitive and improve their own technology. None of these people want technology for technology's sake."

G.A. "Andy" Marken, American marketing consultant

In this section we review the way in which the ongoing information technology revolution, taken here to include the full panoply of computers and allied electronic devices and processes, affects the way in which your career may develop. There are a number of ways, reviewed below, and together these add up to a substantial impact on jobs, finding, keeping, and progressing in them, and on the whole world of work generally.

NEGATIVE IMPACT ON JOBS

Technological change is not wholly a power for good. Consider, for example, one undisputed fact.

» *Technology destroys jobs*: Certainly it does. In several ways. First, in terms of products. If you are offered a job in a company making telexes (or even faxes, perhaps, in the long term) think carefully before accepting – or, better still, look elsewhere. Secondly, in terms of processes, think of the many manual systems replaced by computer systems. It serves no purpose to compile long lists of examples of this, not least because the trend continues and any list would quickly date.

There are also gray areas, effects that have good and bad in them. Let us be positive, however, and review other matters, taking a bullish line with them.

POSITIVE IMPACT ON JOBS

Here there are a number of points to watch.

» *Technology changes jobs*: This primarily takes the form of computer or other technological elements being *added* to jobs. Look no further than the many financial centers where traders and others are impotent without being wired in, as it were, to the complex systems that now keep their operations running.

» *Technology creates new jobs*: These may come about for several different reasons, as the following examples will illustrate.

   » *New products* arising from the possibilities provided by new technology are legion. It is not so long ago that things like mobile telephones, personal organizers and handheld computers, Internet televisions and a plethora of gadgets and gizmos did not exist. It would be a rash person who would predict what will be added to such a list over even the next five or ten years (and I write this on the day that the first space tourist has arrived home successfully – and ecstatic!). All such developments need people of all sorts to develop, test, launch, market, and sell them (and very often to teach other people – or at least the older generation – how to use them).

   » *New processes* also are all around us. Literally. Whether it is your car being serviced largely by being plugged into a diagnostic machine; a smartcard processing a purchase and passing on your details so that, in due course, you receive a promotional coupon from a company offering a rival brand to that which you have just bought; or you preparing slides for a presentation and then just sending them off electronically, doing nothing more until you stand at the lectern and press a button – all such new processes need people to conceive them and make them work. Again, the future will be as different from what occurs now as the examples above are different from what happened not so very long ago.

   » *New business methods* are also a creator of new jobs. When the banks began to move away from operating predominately through branches to having customers deal with them by post, telephone, or over the Internet, a host of new jobs were created in the centers from which these new operations were run. Although many such jobs are essentially "clerical," managers and specialists were needed too.

» *New businesses* must also be considered, though one must be careful of the definition of the term "new business." One category would seem to be the dot-com companies, but many of these are only new ways of delivering what was previously done some other way. Amazon sell the same books as Waterstone's and Barnes & Noble, they just do it in a different way (now copied, of course, by conventional retailers). This change creates new jobs, but some would say it is hardly a new business. Other recent companies do new things and really are new businesses: the business and job of the man who mends my computer did not exist before computers came on the scene.

For some people there are opportunities right here in the new work to be done, for others the effect is further removed, but these dynamic changes – the process continues – certainly open a variety of doorways.

CHANGES TO BEING EMPLOYED

In addition to changing existing jobs, and creating new ones, technology has effects on people in work. There are three main areas to consider.

» *Changing requirements for expertise*: The range of skills now needed by many people, at all levels, has increased. Few jobs need no computer (or keyboard) skills at all. In some it is vital.
» *Changing necessity to update expertise*: The very nature of the "new skills" is more transient than in the past; certainly it needs regular updating – one change here is that a greater percentage of working time is spent on this (and some may have to be personal time).
» *Changing working practices*: This covers things that are, in a sense, peripheral to technology. One example with more ramifications than one might think at first sight is that of e-mail. Communication has not just added a fast new method to its list of options, it has been changed radically, and new considerations arise regarding all sorts of details; for example, is e-mail the best way to chase overdue payments?

In addition, it is worth noting that it is the march of technology that has led to more people working freelance from home, or otherwise on a small scale. If most of the face you present to the world is electronic, who is to know if a message emanates from a multinational corporation or from someone's kitchen table? A whole new range of employment options – and non-employed work options for that matter – has joined the scene.

THE RISE OF KNOWLEDGE

Alongside the e-revolution another phrase has come into the language, that of "knowledge workers," those who use knowledge or expertise to create competitive advantage for their organizations. Such roles will become, indeed are becoming, those which companies pay highest for and go to the greatest trouble to retain.

CHANGES TO MAKING PROGRESS

A further area of change directly affects career management and the tasks that the process involves. The consequences are manifested in various ways.

» *People*: Making and maintaining contact is now largely technology-based. Who now does not have more e-mails than face to face encounters and meetings? Networking, communications, forging alliances, and keeping tabs on potential adversaries have all changed. The new ways need to be recognized and utilized to advantage.
» *Facts*: There is good and bad here. On the one hand we seem to have "information overload" and sorting the wheat from the chaff, so to speak, is a problem for many people. Skill needs to be deployed to keep up to date, to concentrate on the proportion of relevant information that matters and do so without wasting precious time. On the other hand, many kinds of information are available more easily and faster than ever before. Want to research a potential future employer? Just check their Website.

Again, it is easy in light of current developments to imagine that there are many more changes to come in this area.

Meanwhile, even the simplest technology can address areas important to career management with speed and precision. For example, word-processing allows a CV or other record to be updated without completely redoing the document. And new possibilities occur every day. For example, in the specialist area of marketing professional services a Website linked to the journal *Professional Marketing* allows you to check out your "recruitability." Visit www.smcrecruit.co.uk and you can take an online test designed to help you assess at what level you should be working and how much doing so should earn you. And there are more such sites in different areas and industries.

CHANGES TO FINDING EMPLOYMENT

Finding a job goes beyond our brief here and is outside the definition of career management. That said, it is worth noting briefly that technology has affected matters here too. Some application forms can be completed online. It is also possible to take the initiative and register with certain headhunters rather than waiting for them to contact you (try www.spencerstuart.com to see how it works), and there are more than 5000 Web-based recruitment agencies listed as operating in the UK alone.

Overall the progress of technology is having a considerable effect on the workplace, the people in it, and the opportunities there for you. As well as the direct impact, it probably contributes, in part, to many other trends. For example, at present many of those people able to excel with regard to technology are young (remember the adage that if you cannot fix your computer, ask a 12-year-old kid!). This may well influence attitudes to recruitment and promotion of people generally.

Do not resolve to catch up technology, tame it, and forget it. In the world to come we will all spend a lifetime keeping up; accepting and responding to this is the only way forward.

BEST PRACTICE

One profession that has changed a great deal in recent years, and has certainly had to cope with greater competition, is accountancy. In this previously traditional industry, firms have merged, extended internationally, expanded the range of services they offer, and made larger profits as a result. They have also embraced modern technology. Manual accounting systems are now rare, phrases such as "computer assisted audit" abound in brochures, and, for most clients, computer systems have become the main, often sole, way in which they monitor and control their business and prepare their affairs for audit.

So accountants have to be computer-literate. But there is more to the change. The sequence of events, which took place over a few years, in one international accounting firm is worth recounting.

- First, they adapted to the advent of computers. The offered their clients computer-based audits and services, and their staff had to come to terms with the technology and stay ahead of those they advised.

- Then they began to see the potential: there were many new services to be offered if they became expert on a broader front.

- As they extended in this way they needed more specialist staff, and had to steel themselves to recruit this strange breed (and pay them appropriately for the expertise they brought in).

- They found themselves with formal new divisions: computer consulting, computer systems, and more.

- Initially they charged for their services in the traditional manner – by time, and with senior people expecting a higher rate for the work they did – so the technical newcomers were hired out at the basic rate.

- They had recruited and selected well. Clients loved what this new breed of people did, and less technical people (perhaps more senior and hence older) boggled at the work which in many cases they could neither do nor understand.

- An opportunity was spotted. Why should these new, and largely young, people not command premium rates? The value of their work to clients seemed to justify it.

- Consideration along these lines progressively changed the organization, fee policy, and, to a degree, profitability of the firm.

- Now the clash with tradition seems long ago. The new computer-based services and staff sit comfortably with more traditional advice and consultancy, and the "new" people are now as much a part of the firm as any other. And clients seem pleased.

The whole chain of events, decisions, and action illustrates how, with only the catalyst of technological change, the way an organization and its people work can be changed for evermore. There are jobs to be done, and career paths to be followed, in these organizations that either did not exist in the past or are radically different from how they were.

Wait awhile and things will no doubt change again.

The Global Dimension

The stage on which your career is played out can be of worldwide dimensions. This chapter looks at the possibilities for an international dimension to a career.

» International opportunities
» Career implications
» Differing forms of international operations
» Best practice
» Summary

"You don't get any marks for trying; you must actually succeed.
I'm not interested in any sophisticated reasons for failure."
Sir Allen Sheppard, chief executive, Grand Metropolitan plc

The world is a village. The world is wired. Everything is interconnected.
And from much further back: the world is your oyster. All clichés, but
it is true the world is now a small place in many senses and it may
well be the world stage you need to contemplate if you are not to
miss potential opportunities as you contemplate your career. There are
some dangers too. Globalization of industry can have an adverse effect
on jobs, certainly some jobs. Drafke and Kossen remind us that: "Many
manufacturing jobs are being lost today, due to relocation to other
countries where costs are lower."[1]

The dangers once registered, you can regard the international scene
as an opportunity. Perhaps you speak French, or some other language.
If so, there are clearly immediate possibilities for you to consider that
are not open to your single-language-speaking peers. But it is more
complex than that. This chapter discusses a variety of ways in which
international matters impact your career – or can do.

INTERNATIONAL OPPORTUNITIES

There are further choices to be made here in terms of the elements you
may want to see in your career. Essentially, there are three over-riding
issues to consider from a personal point of view.

» *Scale of operations*: If you want to work for a large organization,
then many are international in some way. Conversely, picking an
international firm usually puts you in the league of those organizations
that are large. Product and service sectors play a part in this: soft
drinks are needed across the globe, but some other products are more
specialized and do not offer export opportunities. Such scale also
relates to risk, and this is worth a thought. A large company may be
stable, but it is possible to be quite a big fish in one geographic pond
with a multinational, and yet wake up one morning and find that an
American parent company has made some change that leaves you
nowhere. Nevertheless, the choice of global employers is huge. Step
out into any airport in the world and some of the signs you see will

be familiar – Coca-Cola, Sony, Toshiba, IBM, BMW, McDonald's – all are virtually ubiquitous.

» *Travel*: A personal goal may be to travel. Fine; certainly, being involved with a large international operation of some sort may allow you to do just that. Travel can be also be something that occurs unexpectedly, as a smaller organization grows and expands, perhaps. In my own career, while I neither sought nor expected to travel, the partly international nature of the company's growth presented the opportunity to do so. So now I find business has taken me to most countries in continental Europe (including certain of the old Eastern Bloc countries), to the Far East, Australia and New Zealand, to parts of Africa, and to both North and South America; and to some of these on a regular basis. Most of this travel I have enjoyed; certainly, once it was underway I worked at ensuring that some of it continued. But make no mistake: travel can get out of hand. Living out of a suitcase, endless flights, time changes, and time in hotels can quickly pall, and too much time away from home can disrupt home life and career alike. This is another area about which you may want to form a considered view as you plan your future.

» *Overseas residence*: To experience overseas working and not get the disadvantages of too much travel, another career option that some people prefer is the resident route. Actually living in another country – becoming an "ex-pat" as they are called – guarantees a different sort of experience, though it is possible to lose touch with home base (so much so that you may come to be regarded as inappropriately qualified to work there again). Certainly this route is only for those able to adapt and fit in with the culture and way of working in another country.

CAREER IMPLICATIONS

Looking at the possibilities of getting some sort of international dimension into a career, there are a variety of pluses and minuses.

» *The chicken and egg problem*: International operations want people with international experience, and this may make it more difficult to break in. Other specific strengths – like fluency in a language – may help. Beginning to deal with overseas markets in one organization might put you into a category from which moving into a spot based overseas is easier.

» *Home and away*: There is experience to be gained overseas, and in some fields there is status too. Some people aim for a period during which they work in an international environment as a means to an end; it ultimately allows them to move up a rung of the ladder when they come back home.

» *Long-stay danger*: Certainly you can stay too long in an overseas market, particularly one that is small, developing, far away, or relatively unknown. Your lack of recent experience at home is taken – rightly or wrongly – to mean that you are out of touch and less able in what is effectively your home base.

» *Language*: In one respect, the world divides into two parts: those that do business in English and those who do not. English speakers have more immediate choice as to where they pursue an international career. Those who speak another language – perhaps an unusual one – have the edge in certain markets.

» *The rough and the smooth*: Always remember that there are international jobs that involve a whole additional dimension to home-based posts, that go beyond just getting to grips with a different, but similar, culture. Such jobs may be subtly or radically different. Extremes may involve marketing people politely eating sheep's eyes in the Middle East or trying to remember the etiquette involved in a meeting to negotiate terms when it takes place in Japan. Beyond difference, you might also like to consider a hostile environment. Some countries are not an automatic choice for comfort. A range of things – climate, politics, law and order (or lack of it) or simply inaccessibility – may make them unattractive as places either to visit or to live. For some, this is something to avoid. For others, making a specialization out of one's ability to operate despite such difficulties creates a career opportunity.

An international element to your career may be something that comes, or is sought and found, early on or which develops over time. A few people may get into a senior position with a major multinational, but a greater number may head up operations in a specific region or individual market.

DIFFERING FORMS OF INTERNATIONAL OPERATIONS

To consider career options in more detail, you need to review the range of ways in which organizations organize to explore and exploit overseas markets. Several approaches are involved (listed here in a form adapted from the *ExpressExec* title on Sales Management).

» *Export marketing*: Essentially, this is selling goods to overseas customers but doing so from a base in your home market. This implies physically shipping goods across the world. This may be done by the organization itself, for example, using its own fleet of trucks to ship goods to Europe or beyond. It may be dependant on the use of shippers, whether goods are to travel by road, rail, air or sea. It can be done with no support or presence in the final market; but it may necessitate some presence.
Note: One area here demands specialist knowledge of such things as export documentation, shipping, insurance, credit control, etc. Other roles can involve many different functions: marketing, finance, and more.

» *Export with a local presence*: The form that a local presence takes clearly affects the way a company operates and thus the nature of the jobs involved. The company may have various resources at its disposal.

    » *Its own local office*: This will link with the headquarters and may handle independently a range of things that have to be done locally (and maybe differently from the way they are done at home), local advertising or service arrangements, for instance.

    » *An agent or distributor*: In other words, a local company that undertakes the local work, and marketing, on behalf of the principal. Such a company may specialize, only selling, say, construction machinery, or they may sell a wide range of products, sometimes across the whole range of industrial and consumer products in the way large distributors – often called trading houses – do. Sometimes such arrangements are exclusive, meaning they will not sell products for competing manufacturers; sometimes not. Payment of such entities is often on a results basis, but they cannot simply be set up and left to get on with it. Success is often in direct proportion to the amount of liaison, support, and communication that is instigated between the two parties by the principal. An active approach is necessary. For example, the distributor's sales staff must understand the product and know how to sell it. A company may well see this as an area for support: they provide training, flying trainers out onto territory and taking any other action necessary to make it work (translation of materials, perhaps). Another kind of top job would be to head up marketing in a trading house.

» *International marketing*: This implies a greater involvement in the overseas territories: everything from setting up subsidiaries to joint ventures and, in some businesses, local manufacture. The complexities here can become considerable, with components being produced in several different locations around the world, assembled in one or more main centers, and then distributed to and sold in many markets. Such a structure is common, for instance, in the motor market.

» *Licensing*: This is an example of just one other possible approach. Here nothing is done on an ongoing basis by the principal. They sell the right – the license – to produce the product to someone else. The deal may include help with a variety of set-up processes, from the provision of drawings to actual machinery, but thereafter the local company runs their own show, and marketing and payment is on some sort of "per product produced" basis.

» *E-commerce*: A more recent development is the phenomenon of business that may, in a sense, operate anywhere in the world from anywhere in the world. This is another area of growing opportunity for people seeking an international dimension to their career.

There are also other methods of operating; *franchising*, for instance, well known from the likes of McDonalds, but used with a wide range of products and services.

All these approaches, and more, provide a variety of different possibilities in terms of career options. If there is to be an international element to a career it makes the process of career management just a little more complex. It is another variable, another ball to be juggled simultaneously with others, if you like.

International positions may be senior, prestigious, well rewarded and well supported – a large set-up in a large market. This is also an area where people may find they do not have the same level of support overseas as may be available at home. Headquarters staff may inhabit a large office, surrounded by staff and support services. The equivalent position in another country may only be one of a handful of people. Posting a letter may mean going to the mailbox personally. Briefing a major customer may mean a visit "up-country" in a four-wheel-drive vehicle on roads made treacherous by the rainy season.

However you look at things, it remains in most ways a big world we live in. Geography is certainly a potential decision area for many people thinking about how to develop their careers – and a potential source of additional satisfaction.

BEST PRACTICE

International organizations may well use the fact that they have many offices and locations to help develop staff. Not every employee can move from one location to another, but for some high-flying executives this can add significantly to their experience, accelerating it and broadening it. There are such opportunities in many organizations, and obviously more of them in large ones.

If opportunities exist then people will take advantage of them. A good example of responding to an international challenge comes from within Proctor & Gamble. Below, Myles Proudfoot is quoted on his feelings on having moved from the UK operation of P&G to their headquarters in Cincinnati. A thirty-something marketing manager, Myles was offered several jobs on graduating from university (he did a business degree which necessitated spending time in Britain and France). His choice of university and of employer was influenced by his desire to work internationally. With considerable prescience he rejected an offer from Marks & Spencer who then rated, amongst other things, his fluent French and have now just recently closed down their French activity. So, having worked first for P&G in the UK, he reports a year or so on from his move.

From across the pond ...

"So far, coming to the US has had a big impact on my career, projecting me more into the limelight than ever before. The biggest difference in my work environment has been how much closer I am to the center of power. Being an ex-pat makes you more visible to an organization as well as raising expectations about your performance.

"Being a Brit in the US is generally good news. There's the big novelty factor of the British accent. And having a name like mine really gets them going. Americans do business differently than Brits. For a start, I was surprised how little humor is used in meetings. I learned quickly to drop any attempts at irony; Americans take themselves very seriously. American humor extends to 'would you like to borrow my video of *The Patriot?*' Presentation is important here and the Americans have a much more polished style than the Brits.

"Working here has been different from my previous experiences, as I have moved to the corporate headquarters. I've adapted from a 'make do' mentality to an abundance of resources, people, and processes that need to be followed. Why do it yourself when three others will do it for you!

"How might such a move assist me long-term?

"I make a point of actively contacting the movers and shakers in the company, to learn from them and share my ideas. The network of contacts I have developed and wide exposure to new people is helping me to connect with the latest ideas and opportunities. This is improving my chances for exciting assignments in the future and enhancing the projects I get offered now. This type of move automatically launches you into an accelerated track of experience. At least, I made sure it would before I accepted the assignment. There's also a certain kudos associated with having had a successful foreign assignment, which can open new doors of opportunity.

"Insider knowledge of how the US parent company works will give me an advantage over the less initiated elsewhere.

As I master the inner workings of the organization, I'm beginning to understand company methods or decisions I once questioned before I came the US.

"Lastly, coming to the US has changed the way I see the business world, exposed me to new horizons, and raised my expectations of what I want to do in the future.

"Going back to my old job in the UK is no longer in my 'game plan.'"

Myles Proudfoot, Proctor & Gamble, Cincinnati

The thinking here has clear lessons for anyone contemplating a similar move. The countries involved obviously make a difference (incidentally, there would be just as much to consider in moving from the States to the UK), but the principles would be similar.

SUMMARY

An international element can enhance many a career. Consider it carefully, however.

» Think through the advantages and the disadvantages – do you really want to live in Lagos or live out of a suitcase for six months of the year?

» If you decide on specific objectives, include them in your career plan, and, if they are important, make them a priority.

» Be careful not to let consideration of minor or transient international matters (e.g. another trip to New York) take up disproportionate time and effort; at worst it could make you miss out on other, more important, factors.

» Beware of the possibility that things seen as international perks (attending a conference in Singapore) may kick-start the political machine, as people vie with each other to be selected. Some may just want the trip, others may see it as a means to an end – and some could be sent to get them *away* from something else!

» When successful, link, record, and use your international experience, incorporating it into every appropriate element, from CV to appraisal.

NOTE

1 Drafke, M.W. and Kossen, S. (1998) *The Human Side of Organizations*, 7th edn. Addison-Wesley, Reading, MA.

The State of the Art

The idea of career management may seem logical – indeed necessary – but what exactly does it entail in terms of action? This chapter looks at the key processes involved.

» Analysis on which to base career intentions
» Research to assist your progress
» Action – an action plan
» Qualifications
» Personal rules
    » Communications
    » People power
    » Training and development
    » Personal profile
    » Office politics
    » Achievement and results
    » A management role
» Constant readiness
» New directions
» Going it alone
» Summary

"Confidence is something rooted in the unpleasant, harsh aspects of life and not in warmth and safety. It is an intangible quality, but it has its own momentum. The longer you are able to survive and succeed the better you are able to further survive and succeed."

An Wang, founder, Wang Laboratories

Career management is essentially an individually motivated and initiated process. Of course, other people will help, or can be persuaded to, and in some organizations certain specific help is provided. In reviewing now what constitutes career management in terms of action, this should be borne in mind. If *you* are not managing your career – and doing so actively and on an ongoing basis – then *no one* is managing it. It is a little like being adrift in a boat. It *may* move in the direction you want and find safety on shore, but assuming so is putting a lot of faith in prevailing currents and ignoring the possibility of rocks. Better to fire up the outboard.

So the message is clear: you must take the initiative. The logic here may be clear, but the day to day situation does not help. You may feel you are too busy just holding down the job you have and trying to deliver the results with which you are charged to deliver. There is no time for anything else. But the moment passes. As this chapter makes clear, all the tactics you can employ need working at on an ongoing basis. You cannot regard career management as something to be done only as and when time allows. Not least this is because what needs to be done must often link into events over which you have no control. For example, you cannot resolve to make particular use of an annual job appraisal meeting after it has been held; you are either ready for it on its due date, or not.

There are three clear parts to the career management process:

» analysis;
» research; and
» action.

The third must clearly continue throughout your career, the other two are also processes that, if not continuous, certainly need revisiting from time to time.

ANALYSIS ON WHICH TO BASE CAREER INTENTIONS

There are several stages of thinking that are useful.

» *Assess your skills*: You may be surprised how many you have, including, for example:
  » communicating;
  » influencing;
  » managing (people or projects);
  » problem solving;
  » creativity;
  » social skills;
  » numeracy; and
  » special skills (everything from languages to computer usage).
» *Assess your work values*: Here you should consider factors such as having a:
  » strong need to achieve;
  » need for a high salary;
  » high job satisfaction requirement;
  » liking for doing something "worthwhile;" and
  » desire to be creative.

There may be many other factors here, from wanting opportunities to travel, to being independent in the way you work or preferring to operate as part of a team.

» *Assess your personal characteristics*: Here you consider such factors as whether you are:
  » a risk taker;
  » an innovator;
  » someone who can work under pressure; or
  » a perfectionist.

Consider what kind of person you are and how these characteristics affect your work situation.

» *Assess your non-work characteristics*: Considering such factors as:
  » family commitments;
  » where you want to live;
  » how much time you are happy to spend away from home;

» social patterns; and
» outside interests.

Time is a crucial factor here, together with the kind of balance you see as necessary for you between the work and non-work elements of life.

» *Match your analysis to the market demands*: In other words, consider how well your overall capabilities and characteristics fit current market opportunities. This avoids you seeking out a route that is doomed before it starts. If, for instance, anything to do with computers throws you, then you either have to learn to cope with it, or avoid areas of work dependent on a high degree of computer literacy. While you need to acknowledge what you want and would be unhappy without, you also need a measure of hard-nosed realism in considering this.

» *Consider the picture so far vis-à-vis rewards*: This may have come up along the way, but is worth separate consideration and it may be worth reviewing your attitude to different elements of the remuneration package separately: salary, bonuses, profit share, share schemes, cars, and specific perks (I wonder how many people work for banks because of the special mortgage loans they often give?).

With all the information and feelings that the analysis so far will engender, you can now move on to phase two. There are three areas to consider.

» *Your ideal job*: Here consider such things as your preferred:
 » area of work – tasks, responsibilities, etc.;
 » people situation – many/few, managing others, in a team, etc.;
 » working environment – large or small organization, big city location, etc.;
 » home location – and its location relative to work; and
 » rewards.

Note: If, at this point, you are undecided as to what is an ideal job, you may want to consider formal career guidance. There are agencies that are very helpful, and psychometric tests that can show what would suit you with some real accuracy. This is something you may want to investigate further.

» *Match your ideal with the market possibilities*: Here you may have difficult decisions to make in matching your wishes, your strengths, and the real possibilities in the market. On the one hand it is good to aim high, on the other you may waste time and effort on something that can never be achieved. Not easy, but it is wise advice never to cut off options for no good reason. There is no reason why a more far-out goal cannot be kept on the back burner in case it becomes more achievable in the future.

» *Set clear objectives*: This means *specific* objectives. They have to assist you in a directional sense. If you simply say: "I want to earn lots of money," this does not set out a route to help you do so. Treat objectives as *desirable results* ("I plan to earn X amount by the age of 35"), and then you have a chance to match clear objectives with a clear and workable plan to help you get to them.

RESEARCH TO ASSIST YOUR PROGRESS

There is an important point to accept here, and it is one reinforced by the old saying that "information is power." Your career plan can only succeed if it is based on fact. So, you may need to know:

» what prevailing salary levels are in a particular function or industry;
» how many companies operate in a certain field or are located in a particular town; or
» what qualifications are normally essential entry requirements in your kind of job in your location.

Whatever it is, check, check carefully and, if necessary, check again. Sources have never been more prolific. If it needs a telephone call, a visit to a good business library or an hour on the Internet, so be it. It is your life and it is surely too important to base on hunch, hearsay or out of date information.

Listing the many possible sources that might be relevant to research to assist a career plan is beyond our space and brief here, but some, when you have discovered them, should be noted carefully; you may well need them again.

ACTION – AN ACTION PLAN

This is may well be a plan that you show to no one else. It does not need to be written up like a report, but you should have a record of certain things in writing. Keep this safely, perhaps with other related documents and information (for example, your notes and plans to make your next appraisal meeting go well or your draft CV, ever updated and ready in case you see an opportunity and want to respond quickly).

Do not bury it, even in busy times – this plan may be committing you to some action, and a date on which it should be done, that needs remembering.

Your plan can only list specifics:

» goals you set yourself (e.g. to be on the board by the end of the year);
» stepping stones along the way (e.g. to join a management committee as the first step to joining the board);
» means to an end (e.g. learning to speak French so that you might be considered for the Paris office).

It may also be worth listing thoughts requiring more work to realize them – *I must find a way to get an opportunity to travel* – and then amending these into more specific objectives.

QUALIFICATIONS

One area that may become apparent from your analysis and which may need attention here is that of *qualifications*. Your chosen career path may only be able to be traveled when you have achieved an MBA or a technical qualification of some sort, or been elected to membership of a professional body. If so, then the steps that form the way towards this (and the time it takes) need factoring in to become part of your action plan. It is worth keeping up to date with how qualifications are regarded in your chosen field of operation. What is mandatory? What is desirable? Where there are options, which has most status? And is any of this changing or likely to change in future? Remember, we live in a age of so-called "life-long learning"; this may mean further qualifications, as well as just training to plug a skills gap or update something.

Note, too, that qualifications can directly affect rewards. A recent survey of one functional category (marketing) showed positions varying widely.[1] For example, senior managers received more than 25% more with an MBA than with no degree, and directors with an MBA received 10% more than people in similar positions with a standard bachelor's degree. Such figures will vary, of course, in different fields, but something of a rule is at work here.

PERSONAL RULES

Your analysis may lead you to make some *rules* for yourself in terms of the way you will conduct yourself. At a point where you are satisfied with your job, and trust the people with whom you work, this may seem unnecessary. However, you may come to bless the day you stick with such self-imposed rules. Include the following.

» Always get things in writing (this includes job offers, changes to job descriptions, promises about remuneration, etc.).
» Never cut off your options until you have to do so.
» Always question the reason, even for good things (you need to understand what is going on and why).
» Check regularly to ensure that you know how your situation compares (for example, your salary and remuneration package). This may or may not prompt action – that is a matter of choice and circumstances.
» Record and update your career management records on a regular basis.

Beyond the specific action points to which you commit yourself, there are other less tangible, but equally important, areas through which your career management must operate. The attitude that you take to these areas, and the action that flows from that thinking, together creates a whole fabric of career enhancing and protecting factors. The following topics cover several of these areas.

Communications

Without communications there would be no work, no achievement and no organization. You probably spend much of your time communicating, and every time you do so you not only pass on a message, an instruction – whatever – you also *say something about yourself*. Together with the achievement of your work objectives, this is perhaps the most important factor to influence your career.

So, there are three overall areas to be approached carefully here:

» *Communication skills*: Few people are going to progress successfully in their career unless effective communication is one of their strengths. It is necessary to the job you do and to the process of career management. You need to define those skills that matter to you. These might include: listening, persuading, being assertive, negotiating, and questioning. You may have to be as good at communicating in writing (from a long report to a succinct e-mail), in a formal presentation, or in – or chairing – a meeting, as well as simply face to face. Once you know what is important, find out what makes the techniques work, and learn and practice so that you excel at them. Communication can be fraught with difficulty; do it well and you achieve more and stand out as someone to be reckoned with.

» *Communication intentions*: One of the keys to success in communicating is to be sure of your intentions – are you: instructing, explaining, prompting discussion, persuading; or several of these at one time? Adopt and follow clear objectives and things will go better.

» *Link to your personal goals*: Finally, your manner and style of communication must reflect your personal goals and give the impression you want. Do not overlook this (see Personal Profile below).

People power

It is rightly said that who you know is as important as what you know. People are your passport to a successful career. There are those who succeed by riding roughshod over others, but such an approach is inherently risky (you may rule it out on other grounds too). In career terms it can lose you sympathy and make you enemies, and this in time can prevent your further progress.

Leaving aside for the moment relationships that are simply in aid of getting the job done, in career terms, people come in various categories, covering those who are, potentially or actually:

» *helpful* (actively or just in the sense of being a source of information or advice);
» *able to recommend or pass on information about you*;
» *competitive with you*;
» *against you* (for whatever reason);
» *allies* (in the sense that you work together);
» *mischievous* (perhaps they are rumor spreaders or seen in a light that makes them inappropriate for you to be seen as allied with).

However you categorize people in this way, you need to actively work through people.

» Keep good people records (the day you want to check who it was you met at a conference in New York two years back, you should be able to turn up the details).
» Network and keep in touch (remembering that networking is an active process and a two-way one; it is not just a matter of keeping in touch with those who can help you, it is a matter of being helpful to them).
» Ensure that you have people in place for specific purposes. Who do you turn to when you need advice or assistance on some particular matter? Do you have a mentor(s)?

Your relationship with others is key to your success; never become so busy or self-centered that you lose touch with those you need to work with or keep tabs on.

Training and development

We live in dynamic times and no one is likely to succeed long-term if they rest on their laurels and believe they need to learn nothing new. Remember the saying (attributed to John Wooden): *"It's what you learn after you know it all that counts."*

In most organizations, training is regarded as a "good thing." It is also something that is susceptible to change; often, when sales are down, no one goes on courses and the training budget declines. It is not good career management to wait until training comes to you. The way you approach it is important, and like so much else it demands an active approach. You can usefully:

» analyze your competencies, recognize weaknesses (and new skills that will be necessary in future), and resolve to take action to bring yourself up to scratch;

» use the system – for example, use any resource center or facilities provided, take a constructive approach to appraisal, and liaise constructively with HR or training departments or anyone else that can help;

» take individual action – do not wait for formal action (e.g. attending a course) to be approved, do other things, which may range from reading a book to seeking out a mentor; and

» recognize that all this is a continuous process – not only are there new skills coming along all the time that need adding to your portfolio of competencies (witness IT alone), but many skills change in their application and need to be kept up to date.

There is an overlap here with what has already been said about qualifications.

Personal profile

Whatever your level of self-confidence, and even if you may feel you are obviously destined for the top, you should work at presenting the right profile. This is not a question of defrauding people and pretending to be something you are not – acting out a persona that is not really you. It is a question of making your strengths clear and perhaps making them more obvious. First, you have to decide what sort of person you want to be seen as being. This needs some analysis. It is no good saying: "I must be seen as a professional operator." What does that mean?

You may decide it means you should be seen as: experienced, expert, a good communicator, good (and perhaps patient) with people, an innovator, creative, good with attention to detail, empathic, caring, sincere – and more. You decide, but the list must make sense in terms of what you do, what you want to do, and the environment in which you work. Thus two things are key here:

» deciding the profile you want; and
» actively working at putting it over.

For example, if you write well (or can learn to) and it is important that this skill is in evidence, then you may need to contrive projects that provide an opportunity to use this communication skill. If your impressive reports are then seen by those in a position to make decisions about other things that you might do in future, that may help you. In many situations it is sensible to ask yourself not just: "Can I do this?" but: "If I do it, and do it well, how will I appear?" Everyday activities will allow you to consciously build a positive image.

Office politics

The office without office politics does not exist. As it has an effect on you, you need to understand it and get involved, and perhaps control it, in the right sort of way. The situation here is that there are those that see a side of working in an organization that has little to do with getting the work done. Work provides, after all, a social environment and it is unsurprising if people react to that, but sometimes the effects are negative. Rumors are one example. There is apparently nothing that some people like more than feeding the rumor mill. So, with an eye on your profile and your career, you should:

» understand what goes on. If you remain aloof and detached from it all you may both miss opportunities and, worse, miss problems or attacks – let us not forget that corporate life is competitive – that may adversely affect you; and
» use the situation appropriately. You should probably not join the rumor mongers, and certainly not be seen as a rumor starter, but you should, for example, be plugged in to the grapevine or again you may miss out.

This area can be a minefield. Care is essential in terms of both what you do and what is, or may, be done to you. If you stay ahead of the game you can act accordingly, and in time. Remember the graffiti – *It is difficult to see the writing on the wall, when your back's to it.*

Achievement and results

There is only one, but strong, message to bear in mind here. It is a truism that *you should never confuse activity with achievement.* For the most part, the opportunities in corporate life come largely from achieving what is required of you. Looking busy, being busy, having difficulties, succeeding with peripheral matters with which no one else seems to bother, none of these are as important as meeting your main objectives.

So, perhaps the most important rule for the careerist is this: successfully achieving your targets (whatever form they take) is of first importance in building your career, *indeed it is the foundation of everything else you do*. Attention to this is a prerequisite, and although many other matters, as we have seen, need attention as part of career management, the effectiveness of all of them is reduced, perhaps drastically reduced, by any failure of achievement.

Finally, perhaps this leads to one more useful principle. Timing. The best moments to press home and initiate action to further your career may be when things are going well. Going to your manager for a raise just after some project has over-run its deadline and incurred costs double its budget, may not be too clever.

A management role

Perhaps you currently manage others, perhaps not. While it is not suggested that the only way to be successful is to manage other people, there are things about management that are worth noting. In organizations many, perhaps most, of the senior jobs involve management. This fact reflects the way organizations are, and it also links to the hierarchical nature of organizations. Of course, there are specialist positions which do not involve this, whose incumbents are, by any measure, successful. But management is a prime route to success in most organizations. Furthermore, adding management to the responsibilities someone has, almost always adds to their rewards.

That said, management is not for everyone, nor is it something that everyone can do well. But if you can do it, or become able to do it, (and you might just find it very satisfying) then it is something to consider. If you reject the management route, you reject a good many options and rule out success being achieved in one of the classic ways.

Management is a broad discipline and it is beyond our brief to review here all the management techniques that lead to success in it (though there are other titles in this series that can help with this). However, it is a good example of the need to link the realities of organizational life to your own plans. Maybe this is something you have to be able to do to get to where you want; maybe you can bypass it; or perhaps it is something you want to do anyway.

Note: The factors described in the topics above are likely to be important to everyone. Working in a specialist field – or the characteristics of your own job – may make it sensible to think about other relevant topics using a similar approach to that employed above.

CONSTANT READINESS

The possibility to advance your career can arrive unexpectedly. It is sensible to be prepared to move quickly. Consider the following circumstances.

» *Internal opportunity*: An opportunity may occur unexpectedly, e.g. a new project gives you the chance to apply for a step up and a new challenge, or an offer is made out of the blue.
» *Internal difficulties*: Something changes that makes an urgent move suddenly desirable, e.g. the section for which you work is to be reduced and will no longer be a helpful stepping stone along your chosen road.
» *Disaster strikes*: For example, the company is taken over and you are made redundant.
» *An external opportunity appears*: You have not planned to move on, but you see a job advertised, or are approached about one, that is too good an opportunity to miss.

When circumstances such as these occur, you may need to move fast. Hence the necessity to:

» keep your plan and thoughts up to date;
» have your CV regularly updated and ready for use (though you will doubtless need to edit it to a degree to suit individual situations);
» be able to find and document any record of achievement, from formal appraisals to letters of congratulation, that might assist action; and
» maintain relationships with any people useful to your career (e.g. who might offer a reference or advice).

There are tasks to do regularly if this is to be the case, but it is annoying to find yourself delaying what should be prompt action because of simple updates not carried out.

NEW DIRECTIONS

Career progress may take you up an organization, or around it (for example, to another division or an overseas office), but ultimately – unless you are one of those now rare individuals who spend a lifetime with one employer – you will move on.

You need to be ready for this too. One example makes a powerful point. Someone who is successful and works uninterrupted in an organization for a few years becomes distanced from the job hunting process. If you have not attended a selections interview for a while, ask yourself – how would I do in one tomorrow?

You need to keep up to date in all the following respects.

» *Skills*: How are your interview and allied skills, such as listening and questioning?
» *HR practice*: What is expected of, and how are you judged by, application forms, covering letters, and CVs, and what style and form suits best?
» *Examples*: If asked for details of work done, achievements or successes, can you readily find appropriate examples to quote and speak about them in the right sort of way?
» *Tests*: Have you studied how best to react to and conduct yourself with regard to psychometric and other tests you may be given as part of recruitment procedures? (If not, read something like *How to Succeed in Psychometric Tests* by David Cohen.[2])

If – when – such opportunities come, maybe as a result of groundwork you yourself have done, you do not want them to go by default. Being prepared, on a broad front, is very much part of successful career management.

GOING IT ALONE

One final possibility for advancement and change should be noted. You may want, as an increasing number of people seem to do, to become your own boss. Whether this means working solo on a freelance basis or starting your own organization and employing others, it needs careful consideration.

Key is the fact that, however skilful you are in your own special area (maybe you are a designer of some sort and want to start a design company), you need a whole battery of skills to run your own show. Even for a freelance, it is not enough just to excel in the business concerned; they may need to understand marketing, certainly they must have some financial acumen, and they must be sufficiently well organized to operate productively.

Describing taking this step is beyond the brief here, though other titles in this series may help you if this is a direction you wish to explore.

SUMMARY

The chapter heading here is very relevant to this topic. Career management is as much an art as a science. It is also, as has been said, a process that must be applied personally. You need to get to grips with what is appropriate for you, in your kind of job and with your hopes in mind. Certainly the process:

» demands clear thinking and analysis to put you on the right track;
» benefits from a systematic, and ongoing, approach;
» needs attention to detail to make it work;
» must be based on a sensitive reading of situations and people around you;
» necessitates good and considered decision making along the way; and
» can be enhanced if you are quick on your feet and ready to take advantage of opportunities as they occur.

A final thought: never overlook the process, put it on one side, or delay doing things that you know demand attention now. One way to look at it is as creating a situation in which you are *always* in the best possible position to be promoted or appointed to something new. Your attitude to career management, and the action you take as a result, can directly change your life and career – and do so for the better.

NOTES

1 *CIM Marketing Rewards Survey 2000*.
2 Cohen, D. (1996) *How to Succeed in Psychometric Tests*. Sheldon Press, London.

In Practice

In this chapter the practicalities of the approaches referred to in the previous chapter are investigated further to show how people can make them work.

» Mary X
» The right attitude – personal recollections
» With a little help from your friends
» Hot spots
» A constructive approach to appraisals
» Changing work patterns
» Real life
» Moving on
» Summary

"If one wants to be successful, one must think; one must think until it hurts. One must worry a problem in one's mind until it seems there cannot be another aspect of it that hasn't been considered."

Lord Thomson of Fleet

In this section we look beyond the techniques that make up the process of career management and focus on the way things work for people day to day.

If you live in a culture that rates career success highly, you can utilize this feeling to establish habits and obtain feedback about what others do. In some societies such feelings are very strong. For example, in Singapore people talk about the five Cs: cash, credit card, car, condominium, and career; no one is likely to forget the pressure to succeed or be unaware that an active approach is necessary, though they may have to think what exactly to do.

Career management goes hand in hand with work and employment. Much of what makes it work is rooted in the circumstances prevailing within a particular job at a particular time.

Consider an example. Someone is asked to manage a project. It is important. There is a great deal hanging on it and it is multifaceted. Something like moving the office to a new location makes a good general example. They may have all the necessary characteristics. They can do the necessary groundwork, they are thorough and forget nothing. They balance all the various – probably conflicting – criteria and document a sound recommendation and plan. So far, so good; then they are asked to present it to the board.

Now making a formal presentation is not everyone's stock-in-trade. They are nervous. They do not know how to prepare, or to be certain of putting it over well, or cannot stick to the time given to them and their performance proves, to say the least, somewhat lackluster. What happens? Do people say, "Never mind, it was a sound plan?" No. They are much more likely to take the view that the ideas themselves are suspect. Perhaps they act accordingly – putting the whole idea on hold or taking some other action. And what happens next time such a project needs allocating? The person concerned is not even in the running. The effect on their likely career is obvious enough.

This makes an important point. Many skills can rightly be described as *career skills*. In other words, they are not simply important in their own right to being effective in the job, they are important to how people are seen and how they get on.

Take this example as evidence of a further point. Productivity is as important as results. Another characteristic of modern organizational life is that everyone seems to have more and more to do. Some people cope with this better than others. They are better organized. They recognize the 80/20 rule – that a comparatively small amount of activity will give rise to a large proportion of the desired outputs. Not only is their life a little less hectic or pressured, they are able to achieve more; and it shows. Most skills that you may struggle with waste your time. Presentation is certainly like this. If you know how to go about it, then preparing need not take long. Taking action to correct such weaknesses has many career advantages.

The way that people approach the whole question of managing their career, and making a link between their day to day work and career, is vital.

MARY X

The sequence of events that has formed a thread during the career of one person holds some useful lessons. Mary (whose present employer frowns on personal publicity and would not allow her name to be quoted) began her career as a fashion model in London. She was successful, but such careers tend to be short-lived and she recognized this. With a friend, she started a small company producing and selling natural cosmetics and remedies. This bounced her into the business world and, when her friend withdrew from the business, and she was unable to finance continuing it alone, she sought a position in business.

She first joined a company in a sales position, and found this played well to her personal skills. In time she joined a training company in a business development role. Not only was this successful, but she found herself in an environment where it was possible to learn, develop, and create a wider involvement; indeed, the very nature of the business and the people in it encouraged this.

Like many people she has now worked for several organizations, in this case all connected in one way or another with management development. In recent years she has begun to deliver courses and her latest position combines business development with that of conducting training. Along the way she has responded to other challenges and her work has taken her overseas. She is even the author of a management book.

What conclusions can one draw from such a career? Several things are clear from this varied, enjoyable, and successful career:

» advantage was regularly taken of opportunities;
» new things were tackled, probably not without some reservations, but as routine; and
» where new things were found to play to personal strengths, these elements were used to progress further in a particular direction.

It is success that followed a plan, though a plan that varied and was fine-tuned as circumstances changed. It was a career that was actively worked at – which was actively managed. It needed outside inputs, particularly training, though much of this was informal. And, as Mary would be the first to admit, it benefited along the way from the generosity and help of others – especially colleagues she worked with or for. This, too, was something actively pursued. You need to look receptive to help, you need to appreciate help, or people will not be inclined to help you.

But ultimately, the success has one root cause – Mary herself. In no way has her career path followed some preordained or prescribed path. Without her initiating action many, many times over the years, it might have been very different – and nothing like so satisfying.

THE RIGHT ATTITUDE – PERSONAL RECOLLECTIONS

» *On air*: I was waiting in the reception area of a London radio station to be interviewed (something to do with small business, as I remember), and got into conversation with someone similarly waiting. He was a technical guy and was going to be interviewed about some environmental issue (pollution or some such, the details do not matter). I asked him if he ran the technical department in his organization, and I will always remember his reply. "No," he said. "But I will soon."

As we chatted, he explained that he had spent time and effort cultivating the skill and opportunity to be the organization's spokesman on certain technical matters. This was done specifically to enhance his profile in the run-up to the current head of department retiring and the process of their replacement. He did well in his radio interview, and I would like to think he achieved the promotion he wanted.

His confidence and strategy seemed to me spot on.

» *Rotten reports*: Opening a public course on business writing at the London Chamber of Commerce, I asked for delegates to introduce themselves. One question I asked was simply "Why are you here?" One person's reply remains fresh in my memory. "I'm here because I'm missing out," he said. Asked to explain, he said that he knew his manager avoiding involving him in any project that required a report to be written at its conclusion because, as he put it, "I write such a rotten report."

Report writing can be a chore, but done well it is certainly a career skill, and reports – any written document for that matter – say a great deal about their writer (beyond their content, that is). His response was to get himself on a course, and quick.

Again, this is an example of the right attitude. He recognized the opportunity of developing a particular skill and acted to correct it. Many things can be usefully viewed this way. The opportunity is not simply to correct something, in this case to become able to write good reports. It is to move to excelling at anything that is both necessary to the current job and that helps cultivate a profile of competence. In this case he was well aware that although a course could help and set him on the right path, he would need to practice and go on thinking about it in order to get to where he wanted.

Both these examples focus on skills that not everyone finds easy. It is worth noting that these may be precisely the ones to concentrate on if you wish to make an impression.

» *Too late*: I have conducted seminars for the Hong Kong Management Association and Cathay Pacific. Later I was sitting in my hotel, chatting to a delegate from the public seminar. He held a middle management position with a large trading company, and he was not happy. He had moved out from Europe more than 10 years previously. He was excited about the move, he loved Hong Kong, as did his family who moved with him, and his job was a real step up, a challenge, and he loved it. For some years all went well. His results were good and he made some progress within the organization.

Then things changed. He found himself moved sideways and made no more progress. Whatever the reason – younger people overhauling him, changing circumstances – he found himself as what is now known as a "plateaued employee." The particular situation of his ex-pat position compounded the problem. He was paid well, well housed and had children at a stage of education (also paid for) which made moving them difficult. He had stuck it out for a while before deciding he really had to move.

He wanted to take the family back to the UK but was finding that he seemed to have left it too long. His experience was regarded as not relevant back home, and his salary and package in Hong Kong were not going to be duplicated in UK (where he also had to buy a house again – now much more expensive than when he left).

He was seemingly stuck. He had left things too long and was now at a stage when nothing about his situation was ideal in terms of the move he wanted to make. I left him regretful, but determined to struggle on and find something, but the moral was clear.

Timing is a key factor in making career management successful. You need to:

» look ahead;
» balance the short term and long term together;
» act in light of real analysis, when the moment is right; and
» avoid time passing, effectively without any real concern for career management, even for good reasons, when all is going well.

WITH A LITTLE HELP FROM YOUR FRIENDS

Although career management is essentially a personal matter, it is not something that you should pursue solo. All sorts of things, and people, assist. Two examples make the point.

» *Resource centers*: There are a number of formal processes and people in most organizations which can potentially assist. I remember being in the Resource Center of one large company (Cable and Wireless) and asking someone what it was. Their reply was entirely personal. They described what they could find and do there, how often they came, what it was specifically that regular visits led them to and how it all helped them. Their use of the place was almost unconscious, an inherent part of their thinking – a reflex. This is as it should be, and is the right attitude to take to other things too – the human resources department, personnel, training ... whatever – make use of what is there. And make doing so act as a catalyst to the whole career management process. Such action can help your immediate job (which is important and is, after all, why these things exist in an organization), but it may be years later that you bless the moment that you spent a quiet hour on something.

» *Mentor*: A mentor helps someone with their job and career, usually informally, although this is *not* part of their official duties. They may be in any position, and are not always senior to the person they help; indeed, they may not even work for the same organization. Find one – find several (perhaps you could be one too). I would unhesitatingly say that mentors (especially one) have been the most important single aspect of outside assistance in my own career. It is an area where, although nothing done will remove the ultimate decisions from you, two heads really are sometimes better than one.

HOT SPOTS

Another personal example is prompted by one of my own books, *30 Minutes before your Appraisal* (a Kogan Page "mini-paperback").[1] One purchaser of this book wrote to me. They worked in research at a major university, and they were successful – they had moved recently from another academic body and now headed up a small department. They had already got off to a good start in terms of the work, and were also thinking ahead in terms of identifying and working on personal opportunities in the future. In one area their thinking followed the following sequence.

» They found themselves in an environment where they saw that the formality and importance of certain employment processes and procedures was greater than with their previous employer.

» Faced with their first formal appraisal, they had bought and read the book.

» This alerted them to an area of opportunity: they had never thought very much about appraisals in the past, rather they had just assumed that as they had been doing reasonably well they were of no great issue.

» This time they prepared much more thoroughly, the meeting went very well and they were left feeling that a gap in their career management armory had been filled.

» Looking ahead there was one more thing that could *actively* work for them thereafter.

The letter they wrote me ended by saying two things. First, that their action had made the appraisal go well. Secondly, that it had touched constructively on matters that otherwise would not have been raised, accelerating their progress and being instrumental in their being seen as professional over and above the way in which their job performance itself was making them be seen. Altogether a good result.

This is an example of exactly what the right attitude and thinking about career management can do. In this case they had not really identified appraisals as a hot spot needing attention, but they were sufficiently aware that seeing the book rang a bell. They took the time to read it and acted on some of its advice, tailoring it to their own circumstances. The result: one more constructive move forward in the career plan. It is a good example and a typical one. Everyone can act in this kind of way, responding in one way or another and taking action to improve the progress they are making by tackling different aspects of the process, one step at a time.

For the record, and because it is key to career management, a checklist setting out approaches to appraisals appears in the boxed paragraph below.

A CONSTRUCTIVE APPROACH TO APPRAISALS

Specifically, you need to set yourself objectives under a number of headings:

» planning how to make positive points about performance during the period under review;
» being ready to respond to points raised, including negative ones, appropriately;
» projecting the right image;
» reviewing specific work plans for the next period ahead;
» reviewing factors on which success in the future depends;
» identifying the need or desirability for training and development;
» looking ahead to longer-term career development; and
» linking discussion to salary and benefits review.

The key to getting the most from appraisals can be summarized in 10 key points, as follows:

1 Take appraisal seriously (it is a luxury to be able to step back and think about what you are doing).
2 View it constructively – focus on what you (and your organization) can gain from it.
3 Study and become familiar with the system your organization uses.
4 Keep appraisals in mind during the year and gather the facts and information that will help your next one.
5 Prepare thoroughly for the meeting, thinking of what you want to discuss and anticipating what will be raised.
6 Aim to play an active part in the meeting, rather than simply be led by events.
7 Put your points over clearly and positively.
8 Ask anything where you feel comment or information would be helpful.
9 Record and action points agreed during the meeting (and be sure to hit any deadlines for action agreed).

10 Be open in discussion, constructive about criticism, positive about opportunities for the future and always receptive to new ways of doing things and new things you might do.

At the end of the day everyone wants to be successful. It is an old, but wise, maxim that there is a significant difference between five years' experience and one year's experience repeated five times. Ensuring that you are on the path for five years' experience, and that your experience, competence, success – and thus your role – all grow, is a process that needs regular time and attention.

Note: the above checklist is adapted from the book *30 Minutes Before Your Job Appraisal*.[2]

CHANGING WORK PATTERNS

The workplace is a dynamic place. Many of the points made in this book relate to what goes on in organizations. But what goes on in organizations changes. One case makes a good example.

Jo was widowed early in life and found herself having to restart her career, moving from part-time work to full-time out of financial necessity. After a long period of job hunting, she found a post as an administrator and quickly found – as her competence and experience paid off – that she was effectively running a small regional office for a large international service company. So far so good; then the company merged with another and the regional office was closed.

Her job, however, was safe (indeed, grew and continues to do so). But she found herself working from home. Physically this was no problem. Tele-working is now common enough, after all, and the company supplied everything from furniture to computers to convert her spare bedroom into an office. But other things were more difficult – particularly her contact with people.

People contact is a major part of career management. Jobs may be able to be performed by telephone and e-mail, but it is difficult to give the same impression as when you meet someone face to face, and keeping up with developments – and gossip – needs working at. Jo faced these problems head on. Now she has organized to spend days regularly at the nearest regional office, and to visit head office regularly, too. The increased personal contact, and greater range and number of people met, has already led to an increase in her responsibilities.

Again, the moral is clear. Things will not stay the same. You never get into a position where you can rest on your laurels, and must constantly react to changes – large (and significant, as in this case) or small. Doing so can not only secure a situation, it can change and improve it as well.

REAL LIFE

A final slice of real life concludes these examples on a positive note.

However successful you may be, the old adage that success is a journey and not a destination is worth bearing in mind. You want to enjoy the journey, irrespective of where it may end, not struggle unhappily for years to achieve a brief period of satisfaction later on. At any particular point you may have a variety of views about what you have done to date and what you want to do next. The quoted "career overview" below was given to me while researching the topic of career management. It seemed to me to be such a lively example of the ups and downs involved, as well as demonstrating a clear and active approach to career management, that it is well worth including here almost verbatim. It describes someone working in a fairly specialist area, that of marketing professional services, but its tone could be duplicated by many different people in different industries and activities. This is what Heather Bernini, Business Development Manager for Barnes Menzies French, had to say (and thanks to her for allowing me to quote it).

Not for the faint-hearted

"I consider myself as one of a rare breed, a survivor. How have I reached that conclusion? Simple really; I have been marketing professional services now for nearly 10 years! Many people outside this unique sector may say 'so what?' but those within it will understand exactly what I mean.

"The story so far: my career in marketing accountants began way back in 1990 when the profession was just beginning to feel the waves of change, but was fighting to resist them. Pannell Kerr Forster, then just outside the top 10, chose to open a satellite office in Luton, I was offered the job of marketing co-ordinator. I still struggle with that job title, as co-ordinator suggests that all activities are predefined and all the person has to do is make sure they happen. Not so! My experience has taught me that the position should be advertised as marketing director, as that is what you inevitably become. Pannell's office is Luton did not survive, for many reasons. One, location – although close to the M1/M25 corridor and even in 1990 with promises of train links to Luton Airport. Secondly, there was no way that business in Luton was anything like business in London. Pricing, and interpretation of just where this firm was trying to position itself, could only end in tears. After three changes in managing partners, each brought in from London but none taking the time to really understand what Luton was about, PKF pulled out in 1995 and went back to Central London with its tail between its legs.

"However, I learned a great deal in those five years. I was a non-fee-earner in a firm of professional people and it was not always a comfortable place to be. I came from a background of marketing Whitbread's most successful brands: Beefeater, TGI Fridays and Country Club Hotels. A fast, buzzing environment full of noisy extrovert people, I went into what I can only describe as a library-style existence. Shut doors, heads down, soft sounds of calculators being tapped. I struggled enormously for the first year, then began to build networks around me to help me survive. Outside was where I could be myself, meeting people, organizing events – in the Sally Gunnell golden era (the athlete was then an employee of PKF) I was able to meet her and use her for promotional events – lunching bank managers and politicians (Edwina Currie was a guest in our boardroom for lunch, and I had the questionable 'privilege' of holding her jacket while she visited the ladies!). I discovered quite early on that the marketing role was very much an internal one as well as an external one.

"You need to get every team member on board, or that is the ideal.

"You need at least one commercially minded partner who enjoys meeting and talking to people and – warning: there aren't many of those in such a firm! – one you can get willingly to make presentations about the firm at events and keep everyone awake at seminars! Lesson number one – if they aren't any good at it, don't let them do it! One horrible memory I have was a post-budget breakfast event held in our office at PKF when I had managed to get nearly 70 people to attend (a feat in itself). All guests were seated with their plates of kedgeree (a brave decision on menu, as the entire office reeked of fish for days afterwards!), when up stood the tax manager to deliver his speech on the budget. After 10 minutes of trying to get his prompt cards in place and mumbling down at his feet for the next 20, I'm sorry to say I began to lose my hard-earned audience.

"Life after Pannells – I then went on to work for Foxley Kingham in Luton, a well established 30-year-old independent practice. Joy! – my first taste of boot camp and all the partners had been on it and got the T-shirts (and the baseball caps!) and hundreds of pounds' worth of training materials – ah, but what was missing? Yes, you guessed it – partner time! They had come back from boot camp so enthusiastic and with every intention of "re-engineering" the practice and what happened? Clients got in the way! No one to pick up the marketing wheelbarrow and carry it forward. In I stepped. What did I find? Resistance! From almost every team member. The 'change' word didn't sit comfortably with people who had, in some cases, been with FK for years and years. Why did they have to do anything differently? They didn't come into the profession to sell. Or worse, ask clients for any more business!

"I really could write a book and maybe, one day, I will! But at the moment this is giving me an enormous amount of satisfaction – and, boy, do I feel better.

"The greatest satisfaction at FK was achieving a dream. Myself, a partner, and a manager set up bds – business development solutions, a division of Foxley Kingham dedicated to helping owner-managed businesses realize their potential – and get a life! (Okay, off the back of boot camp, but still no mean feat, as nearly every other practice I met that had been on boot camp were only paying lip service to it!) I was the one who surveyed the clients and asked them what they wanted from us, and quite simply that was it. Help to run their business, creative ideas and someone to share their problems with. Within bds I would analyze their business development questionnaires, help conduct planning days and finally offer them marketing services for which I became finally accepted into the sacred inner sanctum of 'fee-earner!' I took Michael Gerber to bed with me (only so I could read *The E-myth*) and the book *Marketing Professional Services* became my bible.

"Last November, whilst on a Steve Pipe 'Added Value Master-class' conference, I unwittingly chatted to two partners from Barnes Menzies French, a business advisory group in Milton Keynes, in the bar before dinner. Later, in January, they were to headhunt me to join their practice. It took many months of soul searching before I finally arrived here in July this year. They haven't had a business development manager before, so I am going through the entire process again and quite often asking myself 'why??' but coming up with the same answer. Someone has to do it, so it might as well be me! There are still too few people who do this job for professional services, which makes those of us who do a very wanted commodity. That, however, is not enough in itself. You have to have staying power, grit and determination, an ability to stand up to partners and to make them listen. You are coach to them and the rest of the team at times, and it can be a lonely journey. I plan to get back to creating a business development division here at BMF, that is the future for medium-sized firms like this one. I am still learning, and my job enables me to visit and work with all types of business and learn from that experience. For the future I would very much like to share my experiences with other firms and help them choose the right person for this job, and I think I could do that through one of the ever-increasing independent networks. That is where I see my career path."

Despite difficulties along the way (largely reflecting the dynamic nature of the industry in which she has elected to work), the enthusiasm for what she does bubbles out of this download of feelings so strongly that I felt it should be included as a snap-shot of the real world. Whatever happens next, and wherever she may end up, it seems certain that her career will continue to be a dynamic entity that needs managing – any success will come as much from her attitude and actions as from chance and circumstance. And that is exactly what active career management must involve.

MOVING ON

The actual process of job seeking is beyond the brief here (and may be something that you wish to investigate further). However, a brief encapsulation of key factors is given here to link to this allied area. These are the prerequisites for successful job seeking.

» *Prepare a first class CV*: I would add that there is no such thing as a standard CV. By that I mean that often (always?) the CV will need amending to produce the emphasis appropriate to an application for a particular job. This may seem a chore, but it is certainly worthwhile. Your CV may need to vary depending, for instance, on the industry in which the job exists, the size of the organization, its location, and, not least, the precise configuration of the job, and the skills and experience that it is most important for an applicant to possess. It should logically concentrate on emphasizing your abilities and achievements. Given that a CV should be neatly typed, word-processing makes doing this simple enough.

» *Compose a first class individual covering letter*: While a CV can be a true reflection of someone's abilities, many are the result of advice and some are written by someone other than the applicant (e.g. an agency). Employers know this, so in a small but significant way, the content and tone of a letter can add to the information that is weighed in the balance to decide whether an applicant goes forward to interview stage.

» *Be realistic*: Employers use a variety of criteria to make the recruitment process manageable. It is said that the ideal recruitment advertisement prompts one reply – from a candidate who is both suitable and appointed. This may never happen, but the reverse, the job of analyzing and screening a couple of hundred replies, is a daunting, time-consuming and expensive task. The result is that requests for candidates are designed to focus the process, securing a smaller number of applicants from those who are exclusively "on-spec." It is not always the case that someone who is not, say, a graduate – to take a simple factor – could not do the job and would never be appointed. Rather, it is that when an employer says they require "graduates only" it reduces the number of applications and keeps the process manageable. So be realistic. Apply for jobs that are stretching your credentials a little by all means – nothing ventured nothing gained – but do not hide the fact that you are somewhat off-spec (it will be seen anyway). Explain why despite this you feel you should be considered and ultimately do not be surprised, or resentful for that matter, if your rate of strike is less with this sort of application.

» *Respect the processes involved*: A good example of this is the need to complete any application form carefully. Read the questions, think about what you put (and omit), and bear in mind that this is a screening device – it exists to make it easier to compare candidates by putting their details into a standard format, and to reduce the number of people who will interviewed.

» *Research the employer organization*: If – when! – you move to the next stage, you really must not go into an interview and ask what the company does! Employers like it if an interest has clearly been taken (it is not so complicated: get their annual report, check their Website, send for a brochure), and the information you discover can help you decide what kind of things to raise at an interview.

» *Prepare for the interview*: You should check out good interview practice (it may well not be something you have done so often), and also prepare for each one. The latter means thinking through what you might be asked, what to ask, making some notes, and aiming to create a link between your experience and credentials and the job itself.

» *Be yourself*: There is a danger that all this care and preparation may come over as a stilted approach. Employers want to know about you, the real you. Of course you want to paint a full picture and leave out nothing that might weigh in the balance in your favor, but for all the checking of details, the way your competence shows through the way you present yourself counts for a good deal, too. Certainly if you appear hesitant or unsure, or appear to be hiding things, that will not help.

» *Be honest*: Research (by the quality newspapers) regularly shows that something like a quarter of applicants lie on job application forms – and then presumably at interview. Put the best face on things by all means, but resist the temptation to say you were studying for a postgraduate degree of some sort when you spent the time selling shell necklaces on a beach in Goa. It should not be surprising that many employers check, indeed this may be most likely amongst those you would consider the most desirable sort of employer.

There is considerable detail to be investigated here, and skills to be developed and deployed. Finding an opportunity is only half the battle, you must actively bring it to fruition.

SUMMARY

To encapsulate the essence of career management briefly is not easy, but the following does reflect the key issues and approaches.

» Having the right attitude – and developing the habit of thinking about the career implications of everything – is the first basis for success.
» Systematically utilize those strategies most likely to produce the effects you want and best focused on your objectives.
» Aim high and watch for opportunities wherever they may present themselves.
» Be prepared in every way to take action fast and effectively when the moment is right.

NOTES

1 Forsyth, P. (1999) *30 Minutes Before your Job Appraisal*. Kogan Page, London.
2 See note 1.

Key Concepts and Thinkers

Further ideas and definitions appear in this chapter, from what is written about the subject elsewhere to the process of finding a job.

» Glossary
» Key concepts and thinkers
» Summary

"Hitch your wagon to a star; keep your nose to the grindstone; put your shoulder to the wheel; keep an ear to the ground and watch for writing on the wall"

Herbert Prochnow, former president, First National Bank of Chicago

Career management is not a highly technical subject, but there are a few terms that it is useful to clarify; some overlap with the area of job hunting.

GLOSSARY

Appraisal (or job, performance, or staff appraisal) – The formal process of evaluation, manifested primarily in the regular – often annual – appraisal interview that links performance in one period with goals and targets for the next.

Aptitude tests – Generic term for a range of tests designed to provide more certainty in selecting the right candidate. Some are more useful than others. You can measure IQ but it is difficult to define and state how knowing it (at least in average ranges) helps you assess a candidate. You can measure very clearly things like fluency in a foreign language or numeracy.

Assessment center – Describes a process rather than a place: the process of assembling a group of applicants for job selection (or promotion) and dealing with them on a group basis.

Career commitment – Term used to describe the psychological state of being committed to working actively to enhance your career prospects.

Career ladder – A formal path laid down by an organization as a guide to how an employee would likely progress; now much less in evidence and much less likely to be a guaranteed guide.

Career management – Our topic here: the personal, systematic, ongoing planning and fine-tuning of objectives and action that is designed to progress a career.

Career planning – Most usually applied to the corporate intention to guide people along a particular path (remember that such a path does not necessarily match an individual's requirements accurately).

Career plan – The plan that states personal goals and intentions as the basis for career management.

Curriculum vitae – This – the ubiquitous CV – is the written statement of a career to date, used in attempting to move on (internally or externally). Importantly it should describe not just the facts of employment, but the achievements of work done.

Downshifting – An intentional move to simplify life, usually involving a move away from the "rat race." Self-employment, job change, and a geographic move (e.g. away from a city) may all be involved.

Downsizing – Also euphemistically known as "rightsizing," this is the term used to refer to a strategy of corporate contraction in the sense that fewer people will be needed for the new way of operating.

Exit interviews – Interviews held as people leave, aimed at discovering why people leave in order to assist in the improvement of recruitment policy and practice. As such, these may not help people in their careers, but sometimes the same sort of thing is done when people move internally (to a new division or location, perhaps), and that may be something from which the careerist can learn.

Fast track – Sometimes used as a formal term for employees selected to be moved through a career path, usually early in their career, on an accelerated basis; also a general term for rapid progress.

Graphology – The art or science depending on your point of view of inferring the characteristics of a job applicant from their handwriting.

Headhunter – Agencies or executive search consultants who seek candidates (usually for reasonably senior posts) "to order," finding them through research and contacts rather than advertising. Informally, any direct approach may be referred to as "headhunting."

Job enlargement – An expansion of work activities and responsibilities. It can be positive or may sometimes be a way for the organization to get more output without paying for it.

Job redesign – As with "sideways move," this is usually a negative term, implying action to keep someone at the same level.

Job rotation – The specific strategy, used by some organizations, o moving people from one job to another as a general philosophy o ringing the changes, rather than because of the merits of an ind vidual move. It is felt to create positive motivation by enhancing jo satisfaction and to stimulate creativity and retention.

Job satisfaction – All the elements of interest, satisfaction, fun, challenge, and more that can come from working.

Job sharing – The way of working that covers one job with two (or more) people working on a part-time basis.

Networking – The skill of keeping in touch with people, or contact management. There really is an art to doing this in a way that is truly useful and yet does not become unduly time-consuming or an end in itself. Stands investigation as an essential career management tool.

Outplacement – A euphemism for terminating employment or "letting people go." Outplacement counseling is sometimes offered to soften the blow and help an individual find alternative employment. If you are ever in this position and offered such help – take it, anything that speeds the process of relocation may be useful.

Peter Principle – The theory, originated by Northcote Parkinson, that everyone in an organization rises to their level of incompetence.

Portfolio career – This is a term for working in a way that allows you to do more than one thing. It is predominantly used in the context of those who are self-employed or in small businesses (for example, the author of this book operates in writing, training, and consultancy), but is increasingly possible in larger organizations as well; it may be a useful first step to a career change.

Psychometric test – Tests, most often involving long lists of multiple-choice questions, designed to measure various attributes as part of a selection process. Many such tests are well researched and are helpful to employers. Others smack of pseudo-science. Some areas (such as testing fluency in a foreign language) need simpler tests, and some areas remain untestable; for example, no reliable test exists to demonstrate people's ability to sell.

Plateaued employee – People regarded as having no potential to move higher in an organization; sometimes a formal term in an organization.

Resource center – A dedicated and specialized "library" within an organization that is designed as an adjunct to formal training and development. Usually a library-like environment, its resources range from books to facilities enabling e-learning or the viewing of training films. Though much of its purpose is job-related, it provides a means for the individual to link development and career advancement.

Rewards (and remuneration) – This is simply payment for employment. The key thing here is to remember that both are umbrella terms and that a plethora of benefits may be involved alongside salary.

Sideways move – Literally, a move of job that changes work and responsibilities but does not move a person up the hierarchy; sometimes euphemistically called "sideways promotion."

Succession planning – The succession refers to who follows people into key positions should they leave, and the concept of operating on the basis that internal promotion is always an option wherever possible. Given the importance of this it is perhaps curious that in some organizations it is taken very seriously, and in others it is ignored. If you hanker after your boss's job, it may well be worth knowing what plans, if any, exist should they leave.

Tele-working – Working, full- or part-time, from home, connected to the office and any other contacts by telephone – or, these days, by telephone line, as this includes all forms of electronic communication.

KEY CONCEPTS AND THINKERS

The gurus have addressed career management as they have every other aspect of organizational life. Two examples, both of whom recognize the fact that the mix of people's motivation about their careers varies, are:

» John Holland, an American academic and consultant, whose "occupational interests" matrix sets out these varied factors under a number of headings: realistic, investigative, artistic, social, enterprising, and conventional. You can read more about this in his book *Making Vocational Choices*;[1] and

» Ed Schein, another American consultant, who suggests that once into a career, people settle on one "career anchor" – an underlying career value that is more important to them in making decisions than any other factor. The groups factors under various headings: technical/functional, managerial, autonomy/independence, security/stability, service/dedication, pure challenge, lifestyle integration, and entrepreneurship. You can read more in his book *Career Anchors: Discovering your real values*.[2]

Such theories are, though doubtless interesting and of some guidance for organizations wondering how to handle people, less practical than an individual's own feelings.

More likely to be useful is a writer like Charles Handy, whose books (particularly *The Empty Raincoat*[3] and *The Search for Meaning*[4]) offer real insight into the world of work and where it is going. There is, however, some agreement about trends that affect people in their careers. The following points are key.

» People are reaching the highest level of their career earlier than in the past (in many cases by their mid/late thirties). This means that the steps up to that time need special consideration; it is easier and easier to leave things too late.

» Flatter organizations mean there are big jumps to make between the few managerial levels there are; this has implications for both organizations – have they the people able to make these jumps? – and the individual who will want to be one who can.

» There are less central services in most large organizations; staff must work hard to get the commitment and support (for example, for development and training) from hard-pressed line managers trying to operate very much alone.

» Lower staffing levels mean more for fewer people to do; organizations must ensure that these people have the right competencies, and support those who do – with obvious consequences for the individual.

» With more to be done by fewer people there is more pressure (and, for some, more stress); organizations have to work to keep up morale and individuals have to be seen to cope if they want to be singled out for opportunities that perhaps inherently involve more pressure.

The workplace is changing and the successful careerist will want to keep up to date, to anticipate such changes wherever possible, certainly to respond to them fast. This means looking at the trends alongside your strengths; and in doing so, it is worth remembering what Peter

Drucker said in *Management Challenges for the 21st Century*: "Most people think they know what they are good at. They are usually wrong. People know what they are not good at more often – and even there people are more often wrong than right. And yet, one can only perform with one's strengths. One cannot build performance on weaknesses, let alone on something one cannot do at all."[5]

Some other books that look usefully ahead in this way are:

» *The World in 2020* by Hamish McRae;[6]
» *When Giants Learn to Dance* by Rosbeth Moss Canter;[7] and
» *The Art of the Long View* by Peter Schwarz.[8]

Remember, though, what Neils Bohr said: "Prediction is always difficult, especially of the future" – ultimately you must judge what is most likely and how it will affect you. Remember, too, that a small change internally in the organization that employs you may, in the short term, be infinitely more significant than so-called global changes.

In addition, some companies have a stated view of career management that accepts the two sides involved. For example, ICL, the UK computer company, has been quoted as having a policy that takes account of the individual (e.g. career counseling, CV writing) and organizational (e.g. career structures, high-flyer schemes) aspects of career planning – and of those that are important on both sides (e.g. appraisal, mentoring). In an organization that adopts formal positions these are obviously key too and should not be ignored.

SUMMARY

In summary, or more as a final word here, the key thing to remember is just how dynamic are the current times. There is no sign of the pace of change slackening, and the most successful people in future organizations will be, not least, those that keep abreast of change and anticipate it where they can. On the one hand your career is worth some consideration (snap judgments may not always take you reliably in the right direction), on the other you need to be ready to take advantage of changing circumstances as they occur.

NOTES

1 Holland, J. (1985) *Making Vocational Choices: A theory of vocational personalities and work environments*. Prentice Hall, New Jersey.
2 Schein, E. (1985) *Career Anchors: Discovering your real values*. Pfeiffer Jassey–Bass, San Francisco, CA.
3 Handy, C. (1994) *The Empty Raincoat*. Hutchinson, London.
4 Handy, C. (1996) *The Search for Meaning*. Lemos & Crane, London.
5 Drucker, P. (1999) *Management Challenges for the 21st Century*. Butterworth-Heinemann, Oxford.
6 McRae, H. (1994) *The World in 2020*. HarperCollins, London.
7 Canter, R.M. (1989) *When Giants Learn to Dance*. Simon & Schuster, New York.
8 Schwarz, P. (1992) *The Art of the Long View*. Century Business, London.

Resources

What help is at hand for those intent on being a real careerist? In this chapter a variety of additional sources of information and inspiration are reviewed.

» More on managing your career
» The careerist bible
» Finding and obtaining a new job
» Other reading
» CPD – three letters that spell career development
» Career analysis
» A "must-see" Website
» Work/life – the latest
» Finally . . .

"My formula for success is to be found in three words – work – work – work."

Silvio Berlusconi, Italian media proprietor

The main resource of the careerist is their own inclination – or resolve – to stay up to date and abreast of anything and everything that will help them positively to enhance their career. The problem is rather like that of filing (a survey at IBM showed that only 10% of material filed was ever looked at again – the problem was identifying which 10% it would be). The answer must be an individual one – you have to decide what will help you. There are common factors, though.

» *People*: Who you know, and what your relationship with them is, is vital.
» *Information*: Action here, from keeping a progressively changing career file to recording useful sources of information, must be an ongoing matter; when you suddenly need something it will be found more quickly if you know where to look rather than starting by thinking about the best (any?) source.
» *Involvements*: You may need to get involved in certain activities to foster your future direction; this might mean many different things – sitting on a committee (or not!), or undertaking something that will force you to develop a skill (e.g. running some meetings to make sure you can do so well).

MORE ON MANAGING YOUR CAREER

There are not a great many practical "how to"-style books on career management for the individual. My own book, *Career Skills: a guide for long-term success*,[1] might, immodestly, be recommended and two other good books are *Plan your Career* by John Lockett[2] and *Moving Up: a practical guide to career enhancement* by Stan Crabtree[3]. Another, almost legendary, title is worth its own heading.

THE CAREERIST BIBLE

The one book that is worth a look for almost anyone intent on active career management is *What Color is your Parachute?* by Richard

Bolles.[4] This has become a classic and certainly it has practical things to say about a wide range of aspects of job finding and career maintenance.

Finally, there is one more area which should be touched on, even if it goes beyond our strict brief here.

FINDING AND OBTAINING A NEW JOB

The skills of actually locating a new job opportunity, and of progressing successfully through a recruitment and selection process, are a necessary adjunct to career management. There are key skills and processes here that you need to know about and some elements of this have been touched on earlier in this work (keeping a CV up to date, tailoring an approach, etc.). Certainly you need to be able to:

» prepare a suitable curriculum vitae (and covering letter);
» perform well at a selection interview;
» ask the right questions in the right way; and
» present yourself in an appropriate way (right down to cleaning your shoes and choosing a suitable outfit to wear).

A final caveat: remember that the point in all of this is not to follow a rigid, standard approach. This might actually disguise your full strengths and potential. Rather, it is to reflect the good sense of the prescribed approaches, yet to interpret it in a way that allows you to make it personal and to differentiate yourself from other people.

There is a wealth of literature here (and see Chapter 7 for a checklist). The following books are mentioned simply as a taster. You can obtain texts that are more detailed or that relate to particular job functions or industries, and it is a category of literature usually well represented in bookshops and libraries.

A few recommendations can only scratch the surface.

Getting a job

» Holmes, K. (2000) *Jobseeking*. Texere, London.
» Eggert, M. (1992) *The Perfect CV*. Random House Business Books, London.

» Yate, M.J. (2001) *Great Answers to Tough Interview Questions: How to get the job you want*. Kogan Page, London. A bestseller, something of a classic, now in its fifth edition.

If the worst happens

And one more to cater for all possibilities, even unpleasant ones:

» Cane, S.D. and Lowman, P. (1993) *Putting Redundancy Behind You*. Kogan Page, London. This will tell you what to do and inspire you to do it.

Networking

This is a closely related area and sensibly worth some study in its own right. Try:

» Lockett, J. (2000) *Powerful Networking*. Orion Business Books, London.
» Catt, H. and Scudamore, P. (1999) *The Power of Networking*. Kogan Page, London.

Note: Almost any special contingency is catered for in the literature; a few more examples give an idea of the range of possibilities:

» Bayley, J. (1990) *How to Get a Job after 45*. Kogan Page, London.
» Golzen, G. (1998) *Daily Telegraph Guide to Working Abroad*. Kogan Page, London.
» Wallis, M. (1990) *Getting There: Jobhunting for women*. Kogan Page, London.

You might also want to bone up on skill areas that go hand in hand with job hunting and job retention and enhancement, for example, investigating, negotiation, assertiveness or business writing.

One further resource to mention before leaving the task of actually finding a new appointment is that of *recruitment agencies*.

This is too numerous a category to list. However, there is one key reference that is worth mentioning and which is the definitive guide in the UK:

Executive Grapevine
2nd floor
New Barnes Mill
Cottonmill Lane
St Albans
Herts AL1 2HA
Tel: + 44 (0)1727 844335
www.executive-grapevine.co.uk

This lists agencies of all sorts and information can be accessed in various ways, by industry or work area (e.g. market research). The exact nature of the firm is thus made clear.

OTHER READING

Articles that have relevance to the careerist appear in all sorts of places. What you need to keep an eye on will need to be tailored, and this is worth a systematic approach: what is around in your office? What should you buy, borrow or subscribe to? The following is intended to show the possibilities by example rather than by providing a definitive list.

Articles

Byham, W. (2000) "Pools Winners: How a variation on the fast-track management development scheme can fill the senior level skills gaps created by downsizing and traditional approaches to succession planning." *People Management*, August 24, 38–40.

Hirsh, W. (2000) "Spinal Accord: Employers tend to ignore the career needs of the solid performers who form the backbone of their organizations." *People Management*, May 25, 41–6.

Miles, L. (2000) "The benefit of qualifications: how professional courses can improve your career." *Marketing*, December 7, 43–4.

Williams, M. (2000) "Transfixed Assets: The competition for labor is truly hotting up. How do you keep hold of skilled operators in an era of low unemployment and new dot-com careers?" *People Management*, August 3, 28–33.

Books

Arnold, J., Robertson, I.T., and Cooper, C.L. (1991) *Work Psychology - Understanding human behavior in the workplace.* Pitman Publishing. London

Bolton, T. (1997) *Human Resource Management - An Introduction.* Blackwell Business, Cambridge, MA.

Bradford, D.L. and Cohen, A.R. (1984) *Managing For Excellence - The leadership guide to developing high performance in contemporary organizations.* John Wiley and Sons, New York.

Coulson-Thomas, C. (1998) *The Future Of The Organization - Achieving excellence through business transformation.* Kogan Page, London.

Drafke, M.W. and Kossen, S. (1998) *The Human Side of Organizations,* 7th edn. Addison-Wesley, Reading, MA. Chapter 5 - Jobs, From Design to Appraisal, and Chapter 11 - Job Satisfaction and The Quality Of Work Life are particularly relevant.

Drucker, P. (1999) *Management Challenges for the 21st Century.* Butterworth-Heinemann, Oxford.

Haslam, A. (2001) *Psychology In Organizations - The Social Identity Approach.* Sage, London.

Moses, B. (1998) *Career Intelligence - The 12 New Rules For Work And Life Success.* Berrett-Kochler, San Francisco.

Mullins, L.J. (1999) *Management And Organizational Behavior,* 5th edn. Pitman Publishing, London.

Websites

What is available here changes so fast that it is difficult to make a recommendation. The following may be useful. Sites like www.monster.co.uk contain fairly basic information - much what you would get in a good book - but if this way of accessing things suits, then they add to the resources available.

» www.marketing.haynet.com
» www.monster.co.uk
» www.peoplemanagement.co.uk

Now we turn to a number of other resources likely to help the keen careerist.

CPD – THREE LETTERS THAT SPELL CAREER DEVELOPMENT

The initials CPD stand for continuing professional development. Many professional bodies, primarily those demanding qualifications, operate schemes to assist their members keep up to date, indeed to provide evidence that they have done so. These schemes certainly come into the category of resources. Participating in such schemes exposes people to an ongoing system of development activity. It acts first as a catalyst to action, because there is a minimum commitment of activity required if someone is to qualify for the scheme. Secondly, the activities involved are educational in the broadest sense; they build knowledge and develop skill that can not only allow an existing job to be better done, but which better fit someone to make progress in their career.

Too many professions and their professional bodies operate such schemes to list here. Suffice to say that some, as in accountancy, are areas where one would probably expect qualifications to be a mandatory requirement; others, for example marketing, are perhaps not. To take one example, the Chartered Institute of Marketing defines its CPD process as the systematic maintenance, improvement, and broadening of knowledge and skills necessary for the execution of professional, managerial, and technical duties throughout a career. Their particular scheme involves a fairly typical range of activities, undertaking a range of which qualifies members in this case to become chartered marketers. These include:

» post-qualification studies;
» short courses;
» distance learning;
» language training;
» in-company management development;
» imparting knowledge;
» attending conferences and exhibitions;
» committee work;
» private study; and
» meetings (e.g. attending the Institute's branch meetings).

Each of these is defined in some detail: for instance, imparting knowledge lists, writing books and articles, giving conference papers, and part-time teaching. In addition, the Institute is at pains to provide numerous resources and activities to support their CPD system and allow people to get the best from it.

While there are similarities, every body has their own version of such a scheme. If you work in an area that links to a body doing this, it provides a major resource that can provide active assistance to the process of career management. It is something well worth checking out.

CAREER ANALYSIS

There is a plethora of companies that offer guidance in some way, usually based on psychometric tests, to help an individual decide for what work their skills and temperament best suit them. Like recruitment agencies, there are too many to list. Career Analysts in London is a well-regarded one.

A "MUST-SEE" WEBSITE

One thing unites many people in business; they are busy. You may well say the word is a gross understatement, but suffice to say that you are not unusual if you cannot find the time to read all the business books you would like. Yet management and business are well-documented areas, and a steady stream of new material adds new slants and new material to the published total every day. What to do? Well, try visiting www.getabstract.com. This provides the facility to download summaries of a whole library of business books in whole or part. Whatever it is you want to investigate or check, this might give you an expert, objective view at the touch of a button.

WORK/LIFE - THE LATEST

Managers are working less hours per week than in the past, but three-quarters feel that the pressure and stress of their job is increasing. Organizations are offering more flexible employment options than ever before, but most managers feel accepting such options can damage their career. More and more people say they are willing to trade less money for more time. Who says? The latest MT/Ceridian survey *Work/life Balance: Whose move is it next?* says so. An article summarizing this survey's findings appeared just a few months before the publication of this work in the business journal *Management Today*.

Work and private life seem in some respects and circumstances to have got seriously out of balance. Professor Zeldin, a management specialist at Oxford University says bluntly: "The jobs that exist today don't correspond to the kind of humans we've become." Facts like those in this survey, and commentary about the increasing amount of time spent working from home and the career choices people are making to try and balance their work and private life satisfactorily, may be useful. They can provide firm facts as you assess your own situation (are you better or worse off than others, for example?) and plan for the future.

FINALLY...

Whatever you take account of in managing your career, never forget that general advice, resources, and ideas are just that – general. It is your career and, whatever it is, you will need to keep up to speed on the trends and events of that area. This may mean keeping a watching brief across several elements.

» *Industry*: You may not want to stay in it forever, but keep abreast of it for as long as it remains important to you.
» *Specialist field*: For example, if you are in marketing, keep up with all things marketing.
» *International*: If your career may stray over national boundaries this extends your watching brief still more.

Within this sort of context you must look ahead, and link your awareness and, if necessary, research to where you are likely to want to move. For example, if you are in market research with a product company, then you might want to move to a market research agency and your intelligence network then needs to encompass that specific area.

NOTES

1 Forsyth, P. (1998) *Career Skills: a guide for long term success.* Cassell, London.

2 Lockett, J. (1999) *Plan your Career.* Orion Business Books, London.

3 Crabtree, S. (1991) *Moving Up: a practical guide to career advancement.* Kogan Page, London.

4 Bolles, R.N. (2001) *What Color is your Parachute?.* Ten Speed Press, Berkeley, CA.

Ten Steps to Making Career Management Work

In this chapter those issues that are key to making a success of active and positive career management are reviewed in checklist style to provide a basis for quick action.

» Consider what suits you best
» Set clear and specific goals
» Acquire and maintain the necessary skills
» Do a good job
» Cultivate the appropriate profile
» Use the systems that can help effectively
» Document where necessary
» Deal with people – friend and foe
» Manage the politics of organizations
» Watch for and take advantage of opportunities
» Be flexible

"More difficult than forgiving others is to forgive oneself. That turns out to be one of the real blocks to change. We as individuals need to accept our past but then turn our backs on it."

Charles Handy, academic, consultant, and author

Career management should, in a sense, be a full-time job. On the other hand it is not all-consuming, you do not need to lock yourself in a quiet room to plan and plot for hours on end. The activity that it demands is sometimes formal. More often, it is simply a matter of an added dimension of consideration during the normal business of getting on with the job in hand. As with so much else in business life, you need a plan and this is a dynamic thing. As Sheila Cane and Peter Lowman say in their excellent book *Putting Redundancy Behind You*[1] (a good antidote if the worst should happen): "Your personal goals should be reviewed and updated regularly. As your situation changes, it is likely that your personal goals will need to change too."

Never underestimate change in this context. Successful career management is dependent on forming views and taking actions that are based firmly on the current real situation. Give it no thought for a while, even for the best of reasons – you are busy, content, and everything is going well – and when you next do think about it, picking up the threads may delay or negate action that could make a positive difference to progress.

So think positive. Never rely on good luck; take advantage of it by all means, otherwise it is only useful, as the saying has it, to explain the success of your rivals! And take positive steps that are judged to actively help the process.

Here we recap and aim to encapsulate the essentials, consolidating what is most useful neatly into 10 areas.

CONSIDER WHAT SUITS YOU BEST

Your career management is a process to help *you*. Success has no universal definition. It is not based on financial success alone, and it relates to many aspects of work and also, importantly, to personal life. The detail of the analysis that forms the basis for career management decisions and action is dealt with in Chapter 2. Here we concentrate on two key aspects: balance and change.

» *Creating a balance*: Career management must be essentially practical. It has to recognize the actual situation about both you and the world in which you work. No one's quest to become a high flyer in computers is likely to succeed if their only experience of a mouse is of the type that eats cheese. Or at least, if they do, they must recognize the fundamental hurdles they must overcome and plan and act accordingly.

In looking at such factors as the knowledge and skills you have (or could acquire), your work values, personal characteristics, life outside of work, overall interests and feelings, foibles, and general outlook, you must balance what are often very different factors and often be prepared to compromise. Compromise can seem a negative thing, settling for less than you might. Here it is simply a fact of life. Things are not black and white and clashes can occur. To take a simple example: maybe you want to travel. Great. Many careers can, or can be made to, provide this opportunity. But it is not all roses. Living out of a suitcase, time away from home, friends, and family, constant travel and hotels (even first class ones), can pall. Balance is necessary. Everything needs to be looked at in this way.

If compromise is necessary, then it needs to be a positive one. A mix that, whatever its make-up, suits *you* and about which you are clear. Lack of clarity, running hot and cold, for example one minute acting to maximize travel opportunities and the next to avoid travel getting out of hand, will always hinder your ability to focus and act decisively to create success.

With a balanced view of what you want to achieve in mind, you can line up positive action to achieve just that.

SET CLEAR AND SPECIFIC GOALS

To know what you want is basic advice. It is easy however to find that a confusion of different possibilities ends up making you fail to concentrate on any one of them. In such circumstances the route designed to progress your career becomes muddled. So act specifically to ensure clarity of purpose.

» Decide what exactly you want to achieve (there is, in fact, a good deal of detail involved here, see Chapter 2 for more detail).
» Keep your intentions clear in your own mind.
» Prioritize them: you may need to decide quickly at some point whether, say, the opportunity to travel is more or less important than your earnings.
» Review them regularly and update them regularly.

By all means *aim high*; it is important to do so. But also be prepared to adjust, compromise, and change in light of the situation. If you are clear about yourself, and accommodate the dynamic nature of the world of work – your job, organization, industry, whatever – you will always be well placed to maximize the possibilities of progress in your favor.

ACQUIRE AND MAINTAIN THE NECESSARY SKILLS

You may well be good at your job and at the things that make it possible for you to do it well. More likely, you have some gaps – things you are not quite so good at doing. Almost certainly you will also have gaps to come, indeed gaps you can predict. The latter is no reflection on you, it is just that things move on. New skills come on the scene – nowhere more than in matters of computers and information technology – and others simply become more important to you. For example, one day your job may involve nothing in terms of negotiation, then changes in the job – positive ones – can mean that this is an inherent part of what you will do in future. And you simply have to understand it and do it well.

The job here is simply stated. You must:

» recognize the importance of competencies and their role in your success;
» assess what you must be able to do now and whether your level of competency should be improved (either to hit a satisfactory level, or to excel and create advantage);

» take action to obtain any kind of development help that might be needed;

» anticipate and predict how things might change and what new skills this might need you to add or augment;

» take action to deal with this well in advance (letting events overhaul you can create considerable disadvantage); and

» make a virtue of the process (bosses tend to respect those who want to keep themselves up to date – but stress the advantages to the *organization* as much, or more, than to you).

DO A GOOD JOB

Two points need to be made here. First, and most obvious, is the fact that doing a good job in whatever role you have currently is normally a necessary foundation to progress. There are incompetents that get on (perhaps you work for one!), but it is not the rule. The previous point about development is important here, you have to work at creating a suitable competency as well as at managing your career.

Secondly, you have to be sure that your success is noticed. You cannot hide your light under a bushel and hope to have people rushing to promote you. Your success needs recording and publicizing.

» Keep a personal record of your successes, and keep it in writing (together with any documentation). This is invaluable for a number of reasons, internal and external. Two key ones are preparing for appraisals and keeping your CV up to date.

» Seek opportunities to publicize your successes, something that can involve every communications channel that exists, from grapevine to formal meetings.

But there is an important caveat here: undertake this activity on a carefully considered basis. The line between gradually giving people – the right people – a building picture that makes them aware of how you are doing, and what you can do, and being seen as a pompous, self-centered pain in the butt is a narrow one. So think carefully, do not exaggerate in a way that will be instantly seen through or otherwise overdo things. Try, too, to do things that have another reason beyond just saying: ''I'm great'' – for example, you might want to point out how some recent experience befits you to assist with a project. If so, doing so in terms of *helping the project* may well make most sense. Providing information yet maintaining acceptability makes for a good maxim here.

CULTIVATE THE APPROPRIATE PROFILE

Oscar Wilde, who had a quip for every occasion, famously said: ''Only fools do not judge by appearances.'' This is a truism, and one worth bearing firmly in mind. The profile you have within your own organization, indeed around the total range of circles within which you move, is a *significant* part of what may act as a catalyst to success. You may be knowledgeable, decisive, competent and more – but what do people think? For example, how do you come over at meetings? It is not just the ideas or opinions you express that are important, it is also just *how* you express them. If you are seen as having no ideas, no clout or no patience this may be significant.

There is a wide range of things to think about here. However, detail apart, the key issues are:

» to be clear how you do want to be perceived;
» to stress or minimize characteristics in a way that helps create and maintain the profile that you want; and
» to be ever-sensitive to the fine line between posing and simply acting to make good things clear.

Action is necessary for most of us in this kind of area, and a balanced approach is best.

USE THE SYSTEMS THAT CAN HELP EFFECTIVELY

Career management is not all about what you do alone and unaided. Of course, many of the things that help are individual actions and many occur through the normal day to day activity of your work, utilizing what goes on in a project meeting, for instance.

But there are a number of systems and processes that go on in an organization that can help you, indeed there are some that have helping you as part of their reason for existence. Use them, and aim to get the most from them. The following are the two most obvious.

» *Job appraisal*: Almost all organizations have a formal system to evaluate people and help prompt good performance in future. They should be constructive, certainly the best attitude to have to them is that they are – act accordingly and get the most from them (see also Chapter 7)

» *Training and development*: Most organizations have some training resources (and many also make use of external ones). Check them out. Make sure that you are benefiting from all they have to offer; the importance of skills was the subject of the third section of this chapter. You do not have to go on a course to extend your development, there are many other options such as e-learning, or just reading up on something, which you can fit in. There are low cost options that you can get sanction for if their cost needs to be put into a suitable budget.

DOCUMENT WHERE NECESSARY

Think of something that you were doing two years back and consider how it will help you in future. Who was the guy from head office you spoke to last month and who said always to let him know if you were in town? The details may already be sketchy after a month, never mind two years. So this is a straightforward overall maxim to resolve to keep.

» Keep good records.
» Keep them up to date.
» Use a system that lets you find things reliably and easily.
» Review your records regularly (and clean them, but carefully).

Details range from names, contact details and what someone is, does or how they might be useful, to "exhibits." The latter might range, in turn, from a report filed following an appraisal to something you have done that shows your prowess (a particularly well crafted report or a write-up about you in the company newsletter). If you take a little time and trouble to do this progressively, it saves time – and missed opportunities – in the longer term.

DEAL WITH PEOPLE – FRIEND AND FOE

There are two kinds of people that are relevant to career management (not counting those who inhabit positions or have characteristics that affect things not at all). There are those that can help and those that hinder. And it is worth noting that they may do either wittingly or unwittingly.

One person who is important is your immediate boss. As to others, the possibilities are endless. People you need to relate to in some way or another include those in and outside the organization, people at different levels of the hierarchy – specifically above and below you – people you work with and those with whom you simply cross paths. It includes those with obvious influence and those who can help in more subtle ways. And there may be a fair number of them.

» Keep in touch and keep details of people (it is just when you are unable to find the details of the guy you sat next to at a residential conference two years back when something happens to make them the best person to help).
» Network effectively. You need reasons to be in touch, reasons that are as valid for others as for you. Successful networking creates a relationship, and that needs work to maintain.
» Be generous. Networking is a two-way street, you get out in proportion to what you put in. Say thank you and be prepared to take to time to help others.
» Be open-minded about people. Anyone may be useful, anyone may represent some future danger – check it out.

Who you know really is as important as what you know.

MANAGE THE POLITICS OF ORGANIZATIONS

Always remember that organizations are the sum total of the people in them, and that people operate for all sorts of motivations, both positively and negatively. The office without office politics has not been invented, much of what goes on is competitive, and some of it is, for want of a better word, spoiling.

Competition may be straightforwardly that. Fair enough. If more than one person is after a particular promotion, then may the best win and, all things being equal, that is what will happen. But, unsurprisingly, all things never are equal. So the range of what may happen is considerable. There are people who regard the maxim "all's fair in love and war" as precisely right for the office. They are not averse to an unfair advantage and will act not just unfairly, but sometimes dishonestly, to get an advantage any way they can. Others, perhaps seeing that they will miss out, enjoy sabotaging others and spoiling their chances.

In a sense, the reasons for all this do not matter. What does matter is recognizing that it happens. You may not want to open a bush war, but you may well want to take pre-emptive action.

Alternatively – and just as important – it is possible that political alliances may have a positive effect. Even something as simple as someone putting in a good word for you, or thinking to alert you to an opportunity, may be enough to make the difference between success and failure. So what attitude should you take to all this?

» Never forget that office politics exists.
» Avoid getting involved in the negative aspects of it, which can do damage to your profile.
» Monitor the situation and the people carefully to anticipate either opportunities or situations or people to guard against.
» Use the unofficial communications channels and alliances with people, including those distanced from you by functional or hierarchical boundaries, to your advantage.

Overall, don't panic, but try to keep ahead of the game – these things may make little problem, but the stage on which your career plans are played out will likely have some adversarial aspects.

WATCH FOR AND TAKE ADVANTAGE OF OPPORTUNITIES

For all that career management is an active process, serendipity is likely to be part of what makes things happen for you. You are in the right place at the right time, you happen to see or hear something first, events take an unexpected turn – there are so many ways in which things can happen which have no relationship whatever to your careful planning. Can you influence this sort of thing? Yes. Certainly if you are actively managing your career you may well create your own luck, indeed it may well be difficult to trace back the cause or, more likely, causes. Why does an approach from another organization or a headhunter come out of the blue? Perhaps it is the result of a whole series of things – someone you sat next to at a conference, an article you had published in a trade journal, what an external contact, a supplier perhaps, says about you – you may well never know.

So the first principle here is that systematic career management does not just make it more likely that the specific things you aim at will happen, it can prompt unimagined things too. It is possible that it is one of these that produces a real break.

But there may be more that you can do, for example:

» watch out for opportunities, first by keeping a clear head and not getting so bogged down in what you are doing that you see nothing else, secondly by making connections about the things you do see; and

» put yourself in a position to have something to observe: this may involve all sorts of things, from attending meetings or conferences to just taking the time and trouble to keep in touch with contacts who might be useful in the future.

When something unforeseen does occur, do not grab at it in unconsidered delight. You may rue the day. Rather, take a considered view, just as you should of any other possible course of action, and consider both the positive and negative aspects of it. Then decide, and if your decision is to go for something – do just that, wholeheartedly.

Remember one further thing as you do so; work at making your working life *enjoyable*.

There is a danger that thinking about the nature of career management and what needs to be done to take an active approach to it may blind one to one key, underlying factor. Of course, work is the main source of income for most people, and on that depends your personal security and ability to lead the kind of life you want. But work is a part of life. For many people it is something on which you spend a very considerable amount of hours; more if you add the time it takes to get to and from work.

So surely getting satisfaction – enjoyment – from work is a key objective. At the end of the day the active approach that you take must balance progress, in the sense of position, responsibility, salary, etc. against what you get from work in other ways. Sometimes there are compromises to be made in this respect, and if there are then so be it. You must decide:

» what you rate most highly;
» how you are going to see this balance; and
» how you want it to manifest itself.

Then you must direct your action accordingly. You will never know exactly where it will take you, that is the nature of life. However, perhaps one thing is more important than any other. That is avoiding, at some point in the future, having to say to yourself something that begins with the words: *"If only . . ."*

BE FLEXIBLE

Yes, I know the section heading says there will be 10 points! But ignoring this is just an excuse to re-emphasize a key point. While no one should let thoughts of career management blind them to other things they have to do, it does need to be approached systematically, something that this work has been at pains to emphasize. Above all you must remain flexible. The process is as much about reacting to, and taking advantage of, things that happen along the way as about unhindered implementation of your plans.

So, never assume all will be plain sailing. Never stop looking for opportunities. See your career plan, and the management of it, as a living entity, not something cast in stone – and aim high. It would be inappropriate after all that has been said here to end by wishing you good luck, but I wish you well for the future.

NOTE

1 Cane, S.D. and Lowman, P. (1993) *Putting Redundancy Behind You*. Kogan Page, London.

Frequently Asked Questions (FAQs)

Q1: What exactly is career management?

A: See Chapter 2, What is Career Management?

Q2: Why is career management necessary?

A: See Chapter 1, Introduction and Chapter 2, What is Career Management?

Q3: How do I decide what action to take?

A: See Chapter 6, The State of the Art and Chapter 7, In Practice.

Q4: Are performance appraisals important?

A: See Chapter 7, In Practice.

Q5: Is career management becoming more or less important?

A: See Chapter 3, The Evolution of Career Management.

Q6: Can I – should I – work overseas for a while?

A: See Chapter 5, The Global Dimension.

Q7: What do other people do?

A: See Chapter 7, In Practice.

Q8: How can training help my career progress?

A: See Chapter 7, In Practice.

Q9: Where can I find out more that will help me decide on action that is necessary?

A: See Chapter 9, Resources.

Q10: My job is so hectic, how can I find out the key things that matter fast?

A: See Chapter 10, Ten Steps to Making Career Management Work.

Acknowledgments

I can claim no credit for the origination of the unique format of the series of which this work is a part. So thanks are due to those at Capstone who did so, and for the opportunity they provided for me to play a small part in so significant and novel a publishing project.

Thanks also to David Barker, at Continuum Publishers, for his encouragement with my earlier book *Career Skills* (published under the Cassell imprint); certain thoughts and ideas presented here are drawn from this. Writing that book made me think more formally about the subject of career management than I had in the past. The checklist about job seeking in Chapter 7 is adapted from my book *Getting a Top Job in Marketing* (Kogan Page).

Additionally I would mention the many people, too numerous to list, who have helped me, wittingly or unwittingly, at various stages during my own career. Experiences with numbers of such people – even some who hindered my progress! – helped with the writing of this work. My thanks to all concerned; and to David especially, without whom it might all have been very different.

Last, but by no means least, thanks to Emily Smith, who acted as researcher searching out back-up material and references that saved me time and helped me meet a tight deadline. She took on the task at short notice and did a thoughtful, thorough and useful job; such help is much appreciated.

Patrick Forsyth
Touchstone Training & Consultancy
28 Saltcote Maltings
Maldon
Essex CM9 4QP
United Kingdom

Index

accountancy   24-6, 85
achievement   47-8
acknowledgments   103-4
action plans   42
activity   3, 38, 42, 47, 85, 97-8
analysis   8, 38-41, 46, 86, 90-91
anchors, career   75
anti-discrimination legislation   15
appearance, image   81, 93-4
application forms   67
appraisals   59-62, 95

balance   91, 99
Bayley, J   82
benefits   15
Berlusconi, Silvio   80
Bernini, Heather   63
Bohr, Neils   77
Bolles, Richard   80-81
business development solutions
   65-6
business methods   21

Cane, Sheila   82, 90
Canter, Rosabeth Moss   77
career anchors   75
career guidance   40

career management, defined   7, 72
career skills
   assessment   39, 92-3
   communications   43-4
   continuing professional
      development   85-6
   developing   80
   recognizing   8-9
   updating   22
   weaknesses   46, 55, 92
Casson, Mark   2
Catt, H   82
change
   accountancy   24-6
   global   77
   internal   77
   media   16
   organizations   12-13, 25, 62-3
   personal goals   90
   response to   7, 63, 65
   social   15
   work habits   22-3, 86-7
   work patterns   22-3, 62-3
charities   7
Clason, George S   6
closure   14
Cohen, David   50

communication   43–4
competition   9, 12–13, 96–7
compromise   91
connections   9
contacts, personal   9, 62, 96
continuing professional development
   (CPD)   85–6
contracts, short-term   14
corporations *see* organizations
cost increases   13
covering letters   67, 81
CPD *see* continuing professional
   development
Crabtree, Stan   80
creating a balance   91
cultural differences   30, 34, 54
curricula vitae (CVs)   16, 24, 49,
   67, 81
cut-backs   14

deadlines   48
definitions   72–5
development   14, 45–6, 85–6, 93, 95
discrimination   16
dot-coms   22
downsizing   6, 13
Drucker, Peter   76–7

e-commerce   32
e-mail   22
economic difficulties   13
Eggert, M   81
employment at will   6
employment law   15
empowerment   13
enjoyment   98–9
entry requirements   15, 41
etiquette   30
ex-patriation   29, 34, 58
Executive Grapevine   83
expansion, corporate   24–5
export marketing   31

failure, effects   48
flat organizations   76
Fleet, Lord Thompson   54
flexibility   86, 99
franchising   32
freelance workers   22–3, 50–51
frequently asked questions   101–2

Gerber, Michael   66
glass ceilings   16
global changes   77
global opportunities   28–9
globalization   6, 28
glossary   72–5
goals   42, 44, 90, 91–2
Golzen, G   82
guidance, career   40
gurus, management   75

Handy, Charles   76, 90
headhunting   24, 66, 98
hierarchies, internal   13
high-flyer schemes   77
higher education   15
Holland, John   75
Holmes, K   81
honesty, job applications   69
hot spots   59–62
human resources   16

ideal jobs   40–41
image   81, 93–4
information overload   23
information technology
   change   6
   expertise   22
   impacts   20–22
   job applications   16
   job searching   23, 24
   recruitment   24
   trends   13
initiative   38

internal
  changes 77
  hierarchies 13
  marketing 64
international marketing 32
international organizations 28-9,
  31-5, 87
interviews 50, 68, 81-2

job creation 21
job satisfaction 2, 98-9
job security 6

key aspects
  concepts 75-8
  frequently asked questions 101-2
  glossary 72-5
  resources 79-88
  ten steps 89-99
  thinkers 75-8
knowledge workers 23

languages 28, 29-30
legislation 15
licensing 32
life-long learning 42
local presence 31
Lockett, John 80, 82
Lowman, Peter 82, 90

McRae, Hamish 77
management, organizations 48-9
management gurus 75
Marken, G A 20
market demands 40
market possibilities 41
marketing
  export 31
  internal 64
  international 32
  qualifications 85
maternity benefits 15

media, changes 16
mentors 45, 59, 77
motivation 14

networking 45, 64, 82-3, 96
new businesses 22
non-work characteristics 39-40

objectives, setting 8, 41
off-spec applications 68
office politics 47, 96-7
on-spec applications 68
online recruitment 16
opportunities 49, 56, 97
organizations
  career planning 3
  change 12, 25, 62-3
  flat 76
  international 28-9, 31-5, 87
  management 48-9
  office politics 47, 96-7

paternity benefits 15
people
  contact 62, 96
  power 44-5
  records 45
personal characteristics 39
personal profiles 46-7
personal records 93, 95
personal rules 43
personnel 16
Peters, Tom 13
Pizer, Marjorie 12
"plateaued employees" 58
portfolio careers 6, 15
positive attitudes 9
prejudice 9
preparation 6, 68
presentation, image 81, 93-4
presentations, giving 55, 65
private life 86-7

Prochnow, Herbert   72
productivity   55
professional bodies   42
profiles   46-7, 94
promotional events   64
Proudfoot, Myles   33-5
psychometric tests   40, 50, 86

qualifications   41, 42-3, 85

readiness   49, 50, 56, 97
records, keeping   45, 93, 95
recruitment   14, 24
redundancy   6, 14, 82
remuneration   40
report writing   57
research   38, 41, 68
resistance to change   65
resources
    articles   83
    books   80-83, 84
    continuing professional
        development   85-6
    resource centers   59
    websites   84, 86
rewards   2, 40
rightsizing   6, 13
rules, personal   43

scale of operations   28-9
Schein, Ed   75-6
Schwartz, Peter   77
Scudamore, P.   82
self-assessment   8, 39, 46-7
serendipity   97
setting objectives   8

Sheppard, Sir Allen   28
short-term contracts   14
sideways moves   58
skills *see* career skills
smartcards   21
social changes   15
specialist fields   87
specific objectives   41
Spencer Parry, Anne   12
stepping stones   42
stress   14

targets   48
tele-working   6, 14, 62
terminology   72-5
timing   48, 58
training   14, 45-6, 85-6, 95
travel   29, 91
trends, organizations   12-13

uncertainty   2, 6

values   39

Wallis, M   82
Wang, An   38
weaknesses   46, 55, 92
Whitehorn, Katherine   2
Wilde, Oscar   94
Wooden, John   45
work habits   86-7
work patterns   62-3
work values   39

Yate, M J   82

Printed and bound by CPI Group (UK) Ltd, Croydon, CR0 4YY

13/04/2025

14656562-0002